Truth

Truth

Philosophy in Transit

JOHN D. CAPUTO

PENGUIN BOOKS

PENGUIN BOOKS

Published by the Penguin Group
Penguin Books Ltd, 80 Strand, London WC2R ORL, England
Penguin Group (USA) Inc., 375 Hudson Street, New York, New York 10014, USA
Penguin Group (Canada), 90 Eglinton Avenue East, Suite 700, Toronto, Ontario, Canada M4P 2Y3
(a division of Pearson Penguin Canada Inc.)
Penguin Ireland, 25 St Stephen's Green, Dublin 2, Ireland (a division of Penguin Books Ltd)
Penguin Group (Australia), 707 Collins Street, Melbourne, Victoria 3008, Australia
(a division of Pearson Australia Group Pty Ltd)
Penguin Books India Pvt Ltd, 11 Community Centre, Panchsheel Park, New Delhi – 110 017, India
Penguin Group (NZ), 67 Apollo Drive, Rosedale, Auckland 0632, New Zealand
(a division of Pearson New Zealand Ltd)
Penguin Books (South Africa) (Pty) Ltd, Block D, Rosebank Office Park,
181 Jan Smuts Avenue, Parktown North, Gauteng 2193, South Africa

Penguin Books Ltd, Registered Offices: 80 Strand, London WC2R ORL, England

www.penguin.com

First published 2013
001

Copyright © John D. Caputo, 2013

Set in 11.75/14pt Garamond MT Std
Typeset by Jouve (UK), Milton Keynes
Printed in Great Britain by Clays Ltd, St Ives plc

ISBN: 978-1-846-14600-8

www.greenpenguin.co.uk

Contents

Acknowledgements

My thanks to my editors at Penguin, Helen Conford and Ananda Pellerin, who invited me to be a part of this series and who have at every turn in the preparation of this manuscript taken great pains to save me from myself. In the past, I have mostly tried to take the starch out of a too-rigid idea of truth, but they have given me an opportunity to speak in the affirmative about truth, to say if not what it 'is', at least what it does, what is happening in this little word.

Introduction
Truth on the Go

Riding to work in the morning has become pretty pedestrian. Well, not exactly pedestrian, because pedestrians are walkers and we don't walk. But it has become commonplace. We ride everywhere. Doctors and public health officials plead with us to get out and walk, to get some exercise because of our increasingly sedentary lives. Sedentary, on the other hand, does not mean we stay in one place. On the contrary, sedentary means that even when we're not sitting in front of a computer, even when we're on the go we're still seated – in cars, trains, planes – and with our laptops in tow. People used to live within walking distance of the fields in which they worked, or they worked in shops attached to their homes. Now we ride to work, and nearly everywhere else, and we're always on the go. Which may seem an innocent enough point, and certainly not one on which we require instruction from the philosophers. But, truth be told, it has in fact precipitated a crisis in our understanding of truth.

In the past the philosophers, like everyone else, tended to stay close to home. In the eighteenth century, Immanuel Kant (one of the names on every-body's short list of great philosophers) was famous for having never left Königsberg. That made life sim-pler for him and gave him the idea that the way things were done in Königsberg was the way they were, or ought to be, done everywhere, and that where there were differences, the differences were variations on what male German philosophers thought was true. Kant read the travel literature of the day, journals kept by ships' captains, but he never saw the inside of a ship. He was also a leader of the Enlightenment, which emphasized the Universal standards of Pure Reason. But the problem for Kant was that 'universal' had a way of collapsing into 'European', while 'pure' tended to mean never having met anyone else.

Nowadays we don't need to live within walking distance of where we work, and we can go almost anywhere we want if we have the money for the trip. We can fly like birds and visit other countries, cross oceans, not to mention the extraordinary amount of travelling we do through the media and the internet which bring other people and other places to us even when we stay home. We can be almost anywhere at any time, and the faster the trip, the better. The Instant Message has become the ideal: getting where you want to go in the blink of an eye and at the speed of thought itself. That's actually how the angels travel in heaven, or so we're told by those who claim to know such things. The angels, we read in the Bible, ran a kind of instant messaging service for God in the days before the Most High could have used email or a smartphone. Instant messaging, instant travel, instant meals – where will it end? And where are we going, anyway? Does anybody know the name of the last stop, or the one right before the last one so we can have some warning? Does anybody even know how to get off the train?

None of this may seem to have anything to do with truth, but in truth, this non-stop travel has created a crisis in our most treasured verities. Contemporary life, which is marked by modern transportation systems in which we can travel almost anywhere, and modern information systems, through which almost anything can travel to us, is much more pluralistic than life in the past. We are more exposed to others and others to us. We have a robust sense that life is not confined to Königsberg – or Kansas – and that the world is a very diverse and pluriform place. This has resulted in ideas about open-ended rainbow cultures rather than monochromic pure ones. But it has also created trouble. On the one hand it has created social strife, arising from an influx of peoples into the wealthier nations in search of a better life, as well as the exploitation of the poorer countries by the wealthier ones on the global market. Kant, to his credit, saw some of this coming, and addressed it under the name of 'cosmopolitanism', treating visitors as citizens of the cosmos, of the world, which is an excellent point, especially coming from someone who didn't get around much. On the other hand, contemporary life has created problems for philosophers, as all this pluralism threatens a veritable vertigo when it comes to truth, and that vertigo is called *postmodernism*.

Postmodern culture is the globalized, multicultural, high-tech world in which we live. We can travel almost anywhere, see just about anything on television or a laptop, and see and talk to people on the other side of the world without leaving our seat – and if it started in the western industrialized countries, it is gradually spreading around the globe today. This induces a rather different frame of mind than if we had spent our entire life in Königsberg (or Kansas). Given the unremitting exposure of life in a high-tech world to the tremendous variety of cultures and lifestyles which contemporary travellers see and visit, or which visit them, they have developed a heightened sense of 'difference'. Difference is a buzz word for postmodernity just the way 'universal' was for *modernity*, a word that I will use throughout to signify the Enlightenment, the age of Reason that first emerged in Europe in the seventeenth and eighteenth centuries and which subsequently shaped the contemporary world of science, technology and civil liberties. Universal is a modern motif, difference is a postmodern one. Modernists tended to think the whole was a system unified by a central power (God, if you still went to church, nature, if you didn't) where all the clocks and trains ran on time. Postmodernists tend to think things hang together laterally, linked up like a web, say, a world wide web, where it makes no sense to speak of who is in control or even of where it begins or ends. How do you get to the 'end' of the www? Modernists prefer the abstract lines of Google Map; postmodernists prefer the loosey-goosey terrains of Google Earth. Modernists think things are rule-bound and mathematical; postmodernists appreciate the irregular and 'chaosmic', to borrow a felicitous neologism from James Joyce, meaning a judicious mix of chaos and cosmos. The postmodern ideal would be 'chaosmopolitanism'. This postmodern effect even showed up in physics, when the paradoxes of Relativity and Quantum Theory replaced the regularities of Newtonianism, and in mathematics, when Kurt Gödel unnerved classical mathematicians with his undecidability theorems in 1931.

What then, in brief, is the postmodern, not as a culture, but as a mode of thought? To begin with, the 'post' does not mean anything anti-modern or reactionary against the advances made in modernity, nor some attempt (always futile and nostalgic) to take flight to the premodern. The best way to think of postmodern thought is *as a style*, rather than as a body of doctrines; it is an inflection or alteration that continues the 'project' of modernity, but by other means. Where modernity thinks there are pure rules and a rigorous method – in ethics as well as in science – postmodernity advises flexibility and adapt-ability. Where modernity thinks that things divide into rigorously separate categories, like reason and emotion, postmodernity thinks that these borders are porous, and that each side bleeds into the other. Where modernists look for the one big story that covers all phenomena – like all of human history – postmodernists express what Jean-François Lyotard (1924–98) called 'incredulity toward meta-narratives', which became the most familiar definition of postmodernism.[1] This means a refusal to be taken in by big, overarching accounts, as if there was only one really big story to tell about human behaviour (sex, power, God, etc.). Where modernity favours the universal, postmodernists savour the singular and idiosyncratic. Modernists do not welcome excep-tions to their rules; postmodernists think that the exception is the engine of creativity and the occasion on which the system can reinvent itself. Where modernists seek certitude, postmodernists see the salutary effects of a healthy scepticism. If we take the particular example of language, which is one of the places in which the postmodern critique of modernism broke out, the 'structuralists' (modern-ists) put their heart into designing a deep grammar of the universal laws governing any possible language while phenomena like metaphors and metonymies, which stretch and bend the rules in unexpected and non-programmable ways, stole the heart of the 'post-structuralists' (postmodernists).

So if you ask postmodernists, 'What is truth?' they are likely to squint and say, 'It depends.' Postmodernists tend to be a bit incredulous that there is just one thing called truth which is always and everywhere the same, and are more inclined to think there are a lot of different truths, depending on who and where you are; they are inclined to play it loose. Herein lies the problem. Playing it *too* loose with truth is called *relativism* – a point that we will want to keep in mind throughout. Relativism means there is no Truth, just a lot of competing truths, depending on your language, culture, gender, religion, needs, tastes, etc., and one is as good as another. Who can say what is true? Who has the authority to pronounce on that? So the critics of postmodernism fear the worst: relativism, scepticism, nihilism, flat out anarchy. And, truth to tell, a lot of postmodern philosophers have created this impression because they have spent their time trying to take the air out of Truth. In the late nineteenth century, Nietzsche (one of postmodernism's patron saints) said Truth was an ensemble of fictions and metaphors that we had forgotten are fictions and metaphors. More recently, the highly influential philosopher Richard Rorty (1931–2007) said truth was merely a compliment we pay ourselves when things are going well with our beliefs. He was an American, and a pragmatist. But maybe you already guessed that. Classical philosophers, especially Germans, love to capitalize Truth (of course the Germans capitalize all their nouns), while postmodernists generally avoid the upper case.

All this because we ride to work! Thus our transportation technologies are not merely transient phenomena; they are the vehicle for an important metaphor about postmodernism. In fact, these vehicles are not merely metaphors for postmodernism; they are important parts of life in a postmodern world. In other words, contemporary transportation systems do not merely cause traffic jams, they also jam our idea of truth. The fact that we can go anywhere tempts us to think that anything goes. 'Anything goes', which is a way to condense the threat that postmodernist thinking poses, is a temptation brought on by postmodern transportation and information systems. The postmodern situation is to be de-situated, uprooted, on the go. Every time we take a ride on a train, or an aeroplane, or make a virtual visit to some far-off place on a computer, we set off a crisis in truth. Truths, as Jane Austen wisely pointed out, are supposed to be 'universally acknowledged'. But today, the only universality we recognize is diversity. The only thing we seem to have in common is that we're all different. If someone invokes the power of Reason nowadays, postmodernists wrinkle their brows and ask, 'Whose reason? Which rationality?' If someone says 'we think', postmodernists ask 'we who?' Well, it depends on who you are and where you're going. So the problem we have on our hands – and it's a good one to read about on a long journey – is what 'universal' means in a postmodern world, and what 'truth' means where our first thought is that everyone's truth is entitled to its own fifteen minutes in the sun.[2]

Relativism is the main threat to truth that is posed by the postmodernists, just as absolutism is the main threat posed by modernism. In what follows I hope to dodge both these bullets, each of which I regard as dead ends. I will argue that absolutism is a kind of intellectual blackmail, while relativism, which is widely mistaken to be the postmodern theory of truth, is in fact a failure to come up with a theory. Relativism renders us unable to say that anything is wrong, but absolutism confuses us with God. Unbridled relativism means that anything at all could be taken to be true, and then we're left standing at the station, holding the bag of 'anything goes'. This isn't chaosmic, it's just chaos. If anything goes, how will you ever be able to say anything is false? Why not just say things are different? How about '2 + 2 = 5'? How would you be able to object to lying and cheating? How about people who swindle the elderly out of their life savings? The list goes on. So, fond as we are of travelling hither and yon, Anything Goes is one of those places we don't want to go.

I am very fond of travel, but at the same time I want

to see to it that we do not simply run off the tracks. I will defend the plurivocity, ambiguity and non-programmability of truth while also defending the right to say that some things are not just different, they're wrong, and this without embracing the no less mistaken idea of absolutism. So let me go on record right at the start of the trip. I pledge my troth to the breakthrough made by the Enlightenment. It liberated us from the Church, superstition and royal lines of authority and replaced them with civil liberties, scientific research and technological advancements. I have no interest in simply opposing Enlightenment. But I do think the old Enlightenment has done all the good it is going to do and we now need a new one, not an anti-Enlightenment but a new Enlightenment. We have to board the train for the next station, to continue the Enlightenment by other means – to be enlightened about Enlightenment – to appreciate how much more non-programmable and inexact things really are. The idea is not to put out the light of the Enlightenment but to put out a new, revised edition by complicating its Pure Light with shadows, shades, greys, black holes and other unexpected nuances and complications. This even entails renouncing the title of my book, *Truth*, and breaking the bad news to readers that there is no such thing. Instead there are truths – many of them, in the plural and lower case. There is no such thing as Reason (as it was understood by the Enlightenment at least), but there are good reasons and bad ones. I want to defend all of this – and this is the challenge – while not ending us all up in the Relativist ditch of 'anything goes'.

The problem is that, when it comes to truth, all this movement has produced a kind of motion sickness. The more mobile life is, the more likely we are to suspect what we previously considered true was provincial, what they think back where we grew up, part of the local colour of our original location, which gets 'relativized' the more we are on the move. You might say that over the course of time we have begun to appreciate the course of time, to appreciate that things are constantly in motion, and by 'things' I mean *everything*. Aristotle assumed everything was at rest unless something moved it. Newton assumed everything was in motion unless something stopped it. We have gradually come to realize that everything is going somewhere. Everything is on a trip – all of the time.

In the past, when everyone lived within walking distance of where they worked, people led very settled lives, staying relatively put, and thinking of the earth as *terra firma*, planted firmly at the centre of the universe. To be sure, there were trade routes and communication between distant places, but they were slow and immensely difficult. Nowadays we realize the earth is in motion, so that even when we stand very still, or lie flat on our backs, we are still riding on Spaceship Earth as it circulates around the sun and rotates on its axis. We have managed to travel to the moon, to land a rover called Curiosity on Mars, and to staff satellites that circle the planet, even as our science fiction writers routinely imagine travel to galaxies far, far away. And that's just the beginning. The horizon keeps expanding in increasing orders of magnitude, not only in our imaginations but in our mathematical calculations. According to contemporary physics, as we sail through space on Spaceship Earth (which is but a tiny speck of cosmic dust), everything in the universe is speeding away from us at an ever-increasing velocity, which will eventually result in an infinitely expanded, utterly expended, cold, dark and dead universe. That's the last stop.

In the end, we are all living in the midst of an explosion of unimaginable proportions. According to the physicists, the really big trip, the journey of all journeys, started fourteen billion years back at the Big Bang, when an unimaginably concentrated point of energy burst and began to expand explosively until, at some point in the future, the universe will reach the last station in entropic dissipation. That relativizes everything! It makes Kansas, Königsberg, our entire civilization, Spaceship Earth, our solar system purely local and transient phenomena. 'Provincial' on a cosmic scale. What good will fine words like Truth do us then? What we call Truth will be like a day lily; here today and gone tomorrow. We will all have spoken dead languages and all our lives will have turned out to be dead ends.

In the long run, the really long one, what difference will it make where you're trying to get to this morning? This is a thoroughly paralysing thought if you let it get the better of you. If you dwell on it long enough, you'll find it hard to get out of bed in the morning to go anywhere. So it's clear I'm going to need all the help I can get if I want to stay on the move. To this end I will call upon Gotthold Ephraim Lessing (1729–81), one of the great figures in the Enlightenment, who didn't know anything about our postmodern condition, but who said something enlightening for our times, something that will steer us around the choppy waters of absolutism and relativism. Lessing offers us some sage advice in terms of reducing our expectations and trimming our sails to the winds of space and time. He said that if God held out the truth in his right hand and the search for truth in his left hand and asked him to choose, he would select the left hand, on the grounds that the absolute truth itself was for God alone, while his own business was the search for truth.[3] On the face of it this looks like a huge missed opportunity. After all, how many times do we get an offer like that? It sounds like asking someone, would you rather ride a train for ever, never reaching your destination, or would you prefer to get where you are going? It makes no sense. The sum of Lessing's wisdom seems to be: spend your time running around and don't worry about getting anywhere. The man was obviously not worried about getting to work in the morning.

But let's get off the train and switch the analogy. Let's suppose it's the weekend and we have decided to follow our doctor's advice and go out to do some jogging, when some friends in a passing car offer us a ride to wherever we are going. It is a very kind offer, to be sure, but accepting it would rather miss our purpose. We are not actually going anywhere. Or at least, it's the going that matters, not the destination. Now we see a little better what's on Lessing's mind. Truth, our philosopher is saying, is more like jogging, maybe not for God, but for the rest of us, who have to negotiate the challenges posed by getting around in space and time.

You don't have to actually believe in God to get Lessing's point. You can simply treat God as an ideal limit point, whether or not you think there really is a Divinity up there overseeing all this traffic down below. Although the local theologian will consider this an odd way to put it, it will serve the present purpose if we say that by God we mean the one being who does not need to worry about transportation. That is because God – at least this is what we are told – is everywhere. That means that God knows things full blast, everything, everywhere, and all at once. We sublunary beings down below, on the other hand, have to take our truths one at a time, depending on the where and the when (the language, culture, gender, body, etc.) in which we find ourselves. We are always 'situated', and that situation imposes a limit on us; but that limit also gives us an angle of entry, an approach, a perspective, an interpretation. God doesn't need an angle, but we do. Having an angle is the way truths open up for us mortals. The opposite of having an angle on things is a dumb look, just staring at things uncomprehendingly, like the look I've seen on the faces of students who cannot come up with an angle for their research papers. So Lessing is really saying that when it comes to truth, our job is to cultivate the art of interpretation, which is what philosophers nowadays call *hermeneutics*.

Originally, the word hermeneutics was a theological one, having to do with the interpretation of the Scriptures. But what we today mean by hermeneutics is a more general theory, that every truth is a function of interpretation, and the need for interpretation is a function of being situated in a particular time and place, and therefore of having certain inherited presuppositions. This is something of which we have been made acutely aware by modern transportation and information systems, by virtue of which we are constantly being barraged by a multiplicity of perspectives. Whatever truth means for us – in our postmodern situation – is a function of hermeneutics, of learning to adjudicate; of dealing with difference judiciously.

This brings out something else about what Lessing was saying. Hermeneutics is based on the idea that there are truths big and small, some crucially important, others not so much, truths of different kinds, levels and purposes, all depending on our hermeneutic situation. Lessing was, as is the wont of philosophers, talking about a kind of long-term truth. He was not thinking about getting to his office in time for an appointment. His point was that in the long run, when it comes to truth, it's the seeking that matters, the earnestness of the search, the effort we put into it, the way we go about it, rather more than the conclusion. The journey is more important than the destination.

After all, as we have just seen, in the long run we're all dead. Sometimes we do need to get where we're going, and sometimes we'd rather not. Sometimes we need to get to our terminal and sometimes, as when the doctor pronounces this a terminal condition, we'd rather not. But then again, that was Lessing's point. We are finite creatures and we have to try to see how these multiple and competing truths can peacefully cohabit without throwing us into chaos. That means we have to try not to act like God, which is good advice in other situations as well (and which for some of us is surprisingly difficult). That means we should not lay claim to One Big Truth and allow it to intimidate all the others. God might be able to pull that off, but we can't.

Hermeneutics is the art of negotiating multiple finite, lower-case truths, coping with the shifting tides and circumstances of truth while not allowing any eight-hundred-pound gorillas into the room. In the past, before the Enlightenment, the overweight primate was theology. In the Middle Ages (and not just then), if someone said, 'The Church teaches. . .' that tended to reduce everyone in the room to silence. But if ever there were a candidate for a Big Truth nowadays, it is science. Science is our gorilla. Whenever anyone says, 'Science says . . .' we tend to think the conversation is over. So we postmodern hermeneuts must be as bold as brass and be willing to stand up both to bishops and to physicists, or, to be more precise, to the way that some religious people misuse God, and Enlightenment types misuse physics. Even what the physicists call the 'Theory of Everything', the famous TOE, is but one theory. It is 'of' everything, of course, but it itself is not everything, since there is more to life than physics, and we need all kinds of theories.

Nonetheless, the big TOE raises a big problem which pits it against religion as a pretender to the throne previously occupied by religion. It also reveals an interesting comparison between religion and science. They both hold that over and beyond the everyday world we live in, the buzzing, blooming, noisy multicoloured world we experience, there lies the 'true' world, and consequently they are inclined to take each other on about which true world is *really* true. For the one, the true world is delivered by mathematics; for the other, it is delivered by Revelation. The contribution hermeneutics makes to this debate is that, when it comes to truth, there are many ways to be, and we have to keep an eye out for One Hegemonic Discourse (a bully) in the crowd who claims to know it all and to be able to identify the True World. Whether confronted with theology or science, the trick is to remember Lessing's advice about not confusing ourselves with God. Physicists could very well come up with something to say about everything, and theologians might even get something right about God, but that doesn't make anyone God. It just gives them an angle, a slant, an interpretation, and we need all the angles we can take, as many ways to approach truth as possible, as many truths as possible without falling for the lure of something called Truth, capitalized and in the singular, or suffering the illusion that it is we who get to tell truth what to do.

As I will try to show in what follows, the task of a hermeneutic or postmodern theory of truth is to stay on track with the chaosmic play of multiple and competing interpretations of the world. 'Truth claims' come flying at us from all directions – science, ethics, politics, art and religion – and we need to be able to dodge speeding taxis and to deal with all the complexity and confusion of postmodern traffic. The art is to stay on the move with the moving, which is the peculiarly postmodern accent we put on what the ancients called wisdom (*sophia*), of which they professed to be lovers (*philia*) – and on this point we postmoderns also want to be as wise as the ancients, which (as I will show) demands an idea of truth that is nimble on its feet. If truth, as Nietzsche said, is a mobile army of metaphors, we hermeneuts march behind a flag that reads '*Mutatis Mutandis*' (we need a Latin motto), 'changing with the changed'. Hermeneutics is cut out to fit this high-tech world of instant messages flying and twittering all around the globe like little postmodern angels (*angelos*, messenger) and of postmodern travellers rushing hither and yon, in planes, trains and automobiles (eventually, perhaps, in space ships), with global positioning systems at the ready (eventually, perhaps, implanted in their brains). Whither we are going we cannot quite say, or why. But we postmodernists don't treat this confusion with nostalgia for a more peaceful time when we worked our fields and looked up wistfully at the birds above, dreaming of being able to fly. We can fly, and we can send messages as swiftly as Gabriel could sweep across the skies.

Perhaps, as Lessing is suggesting, it's not the destination that matters but the quality of the trip. Perhaps the trip *is* the destination.

So think of this book as a guided tour you have been enticed to sign up for, a pause from your busy postmodern life, where you are promised nothing less than truth. We will be visiting the three basic models of truth: the premodern idea that God is truth; the modern idea that Reason judges what is true; and the postmodern idea of truth as an event, where neither God nor Reason enjoy pride of place. But be forewarned: the tour closes with a question, not an answer, and there are no refunds on the price of your ticket.

1. Modernity and the Eclipse of Truth

Can anything really be taken seriously today as 'truth' if it is not science or at least modelled after science? Take the case of religion (this will be my example here and throughout, but we could just as well use art or ethics). Can an enlightened, educated person today, who has done some travelling and is aware of the variety of cultures and forms of life, think there is such a thing as 'a true religion' or 'religious truth'? Or has the Enlightenment reduced the whole idea of religion to a fantasy or even a kind of neurosis? The view I take here is that the Enlightenment proved too much of a good thing. It largely delivered on its promise to rid us of the hegemony of superstition and absolute monarchy and to replace it with science and civil liberties. Nobody can argue against that. But in the end it went too far. What the moderns call Pure Reason proved to be a new reign of terror over truth itself, which would elicit eloquent and magnificent howls of pain from the great Romantic poets and philosophers of the nineteenth century. Pure Reason has a low tolerance for anything that is not Pure Reason, which is, I offer, a bit unreasonable.

Ship of Fools

Let's start with fools, which no one wants to be. I said before when discussing Lessing's thesis that there is no need to actually believe in God in order to get his point. Just think of God as a kind of limit-case, the sort of being that does not require a means of trans-portation. To get an idea of how much things have changed, consider that there was a time, not so long ago, when I would have not got away with talking about God so glibly. The fact that I can gives us an idea of how much our idea of truth has shifted. Life before modern times was nicely summed up by a line in the Scriptures, which runs, 'The fool says in his heart, "There is no God."' (Psalm 14:1). They did not speak of atheists – that very word acquires currency only in modernity – but of 'foolishness'. To take God so lightly, or to cut yourself off from God altogether, not to seek after God, was to cut yourself off from truth and goodness and beauty, and that was unwise in the extreme. Notice that the psalmist says 'foolish', not 'irrational'. What's the difference? The opposite of foolishness is 'wisdom', whereas the opposite of irrational is 'rational', and the ancients were more concerned with being wise than rational. Make no mistake. There was a flourishing business called 'reason' in Greek (*logos*) and medieval (*ratio*) times, so much indeed that it got under the skin of Martin Luther in Germany, who wondered what had happened to faith, which is what precipitated the Reformation. In fact, the reason all our academic degrees come in Latin is the flowering of learning in the thirteenth century which invented the prototype of the modern university, which explains why everybody who gets a PhD (*philosophiae doctor*) dons the title 'philosopher'. Greek and medieval thinkers were not against reason by any means, but they had integrated reason into a wider and richer concept, wisdom. Later on, during the Enlightenment, so my argument goes, being rational acquired pride of place, which forced being wise to take a back seat. In the version of postmodernism I am advancing – there are, predictably, many, as I will explain – this move was unwise.

But what is wisdom? Wisdom, the Greeks said, is the love of the highest things, all of them, the true, the good and the beautiful. It includes reason without stopping at reason; it includes truth but it does not reduce truth to that which is established by reason, and it does not exclude the good or the beautiful from the true. The true, the good and the beautiful hang together. Socrates made a mountain of trouble for himself by troubling his fellow citizens to give good reasons and arguments for the choices they made in life, and for the things they held dear – which pretty much kicked off the tradition we call 'philosophy' – and Aristotle came up with the classical definition of human beings as rational animals. His works, like those of Plato and the medieval theologians, were famously full of arguments and reasons. But the Greeks never lost sight of wisdom, of a fuller understanding that proceeded from a wider and richer sense of life as a unified whole. After all, we cannot prove everything, and even proofs have to start somewhere, with a premise that is taken to be simply known or evident. It is a mark of an educated person, Aristotle said, not to argue about everything – a bit of advice that came too late for Socrates, who was put to death by his fellow Athenians for all the trouble his nettlesome questions caused. Wisdom included insight and intuition as well as definitions and arguments (the true); it included action, living well, ethical and political wisdom (the good), not just professorial knowledge; and it included Plato's idea that a life surrounded by beautiful things promotes the beauty of the soul (the beautiful).

The person who managed to put all this together, who 'had it all' in classical times, who led the good life, who was a model for the rest of us, was said to be 'wise', as opposed to 'rational' (or rich and famous). It is very important to see that such a person did not pretend to know it all. On the contrary, being wise especially meant having a healthy respect for everything we do not know (a Greek wise man would never have been able to host a TV talk show). So in reality the ancients did not say such people were 'wise' so much as that they *sought* wisdom, or had a love (*philia*) of wisdom; in short, they were philosophers. A philosopher is one who searches for the highest things, of which the true and the good and the beautiful were deemed the very highest. Wisdom means the love of all of these highest things knit together in an integrated form of life, where each thing was cultivated in due proportion. Wisdom is the whole ball of philosophical wax.

You can see that in antiquity, philosophy, the search for the highest things, did not mean an academic specialty housed on the local university campus. It meant a form of life, the very model of living well, knowledge linked with action (ethics and politics) and passion (*philia, eros*) and a sensibility finely attuned to life's joys. Our special task in this book is to single out the place of truth in leading a wise life, the sense that truth must have if we are to be wise, today, in our postmodern condition. But remember that everything we say about the true could also be said about the good and the beautiful, because wisdom requires that the three hang together. The lovers of wisdom can adapt the wise saying of the American revolutionaries against their king in England: if we don't hang together, we will all hang separately. The wise know that truth and goodness and beauty are inseparably unified, and on this point we postmodernists think it wise to follow the ancients, who were far ahead of us all in this regard.

As opposed to a 'fool'. A fool is someone who chooses badly, whose life falls out of proportion. A fool puts pleasure before honour, riches before virtue, just the way nowadays musicians and movie stars can squander a ton of talent on drink and drugs. Why let a passing pleasure undermine your honour, your gifts, your life? That would be folly. Alternatively, a fool seeks a good thing but excessively, to the neglect of the whole, in a disproportionate way, so that it runs wild over the rest of his life, like people who strive for success in their business – which can be a good thing – but in so single-minded a way that it destroys their health or family life, which is unwise. When Nietzsche dared to criticize Socrates, who is considered pretty much the patron saint and martyr of philosophy, he criticized him on just this point, that Socrates' love of definitions and arguments was disproportionate, that he let his love of reasoning overrun everything else and failed to take into account that there are certain things for which we do not need definitions and cannot give reasoned arguments. We 'know' them in other ways. Fools act unwisely, let themselves be blinded by particular things and lose sight of the integrity of the whole, of the good life, of living 'in the truth', where the true, the good and the beautiful commingle and serve as the encompassing elements in which human life flourishes, like the air we breathe and the ground on which we stand. Nietzsche's criticism is also prophetic, because it is pretty much the same complaint that postmodern philosophers make about the Enlightenment.

In the Middle Ages, it is said, the West went to church. The highest philosophical ideals inherited from the Greeks (truth, goodness and beauty) were taken to be united in and realized to perfection in the God of the Bible. This led to a flourishing of philosophy (the search for the highest things) in concert with theology (the search for God) in great centres of learning scattered across the ancient and medieval world, in all three religions of the Book – Jewish, Christian and Islamic. The search for wisdom is the search for God, as the psalmist says. God is not simply good or true or beautiful, but is infinite beauty, goodness and truth itself all wrapped up in one. Everything else that is good or true or beautiful is so by virtue of having been created by God and of imitating God's being, like so many reflections in a mirror. Not to seek God, to turn away from God, was to turn away from the highest things, to cut off our being from its root and source, which is the height (or the depth) of foolishness. God is like the sun, the very element in which we live and move and breathe, towards which all living things turn in a kind of heliotropism of truth, and from which they turn away at the cost of their life.

St Augustine (354–430), bishop of Hippo, the most influential theologian in the history of Christianity and about whom you will hear more as we go along, provides an especially good example of this. Of all his memorable sayings, none is more memorable than the beginning of the *Confessions* in which he says, 'You have made us for yourself, O Lord, and our hearts will not rest until they rest in You.'[4] Augustine characterizes human life in terms of a search, which he calls our 'restless heart' (*cor inquietum*), where the 'heart' means the seat of our love and desire, including our love or passion or desire for truth. Augustine conceived human life as a tremendous journey set in motion by an ever restless desire or love, which nothing here on earth could satisfy. To be human means to be *homo viator*, a wayfarer, on the way to God, which St Bonaventure (1218–74) described as the *itinerarium mentis ad deum*, the heart's journey towards God. Every finite (earthly) good is fragile, impermanent and imperfect, and so is worthy of only so much love. We never find anything (on earth) that can really fill the longing of our hearts, or be worthy of unconditional love. As anyone who has ever invested in the stock market can attest, no sooner have we attained the thing that we thought would make us happy, than we realize that we want more. That is because we are made for God, Augustine said, and God alone can truly satisfy our desire. Whenever we desire this or that material good, we are in an obscure and confused way ultimately in search of God. When we desire truth, we desire God, even if we don't realize it is God whom we desire. That means that the one true philosophy – meaning the love of truth – is the love of God. God is the very light of the soul in which we come to know things, in the same way the light of the sun is the medium by which we see material things. Truth, then, is a function of the light of God that shines on things and with which God illumines our minds, making it possible to know any particular truth. God is not only true. God is truth. No wonder our hearts are restless: the moment the soul makes contact with truth, the moment it acquires a particular truth about this or that, we want more. These contacts spark an infinite aspiration, a desire for God. If, as the fool says in his heart, there is no God, neither would there be any truth. Not just one less truth, but no truth at all. Only a fool would pursue such a path.

Modernity

Modernity, however, changed everything. In modernity, as Kant said, humanity finally grew up, reached its maturity and, as we have just seen, was old enough to get its driver's licence. Modernity means the era ushered in by the twin births of modern civil liberties and modern science, which promoted free enquiry, and also by the Protestant Reformation, which promoted the idea of personal responsibility. It started in the sixteenth century in western Europe and eventually replaced the hegemony of Church and King, of tradition and superstition, with modern democratic freedom in matters of religion, political life, personal conduct and critical enquiry, all contracted into the phrase, the Enlightenment. The Enlightenment means shining the light of truth upon our hitherto darkened condition. So far, so good. Nobody is against any of that. But notice the light of truth now means the light of reason, not the light of God. A lot of the work that was previously done by God is now being done by reason. In its new and less prestigious job description, the true ceased to form, along with the good and the beautiful, an encompassing horizon or element of life (the love of which constituted wisdom) as it was for Augustine and the ancients, and became a property of assertions or propositions. Of course the ancients knew all about true assertions. They were the ones who first theorized about them. They invented the study of valid assertions ('logic'), and created the habits of thought that eventually led to modern science and technology. But they also knew that wisdom is larger than logic, and they saw and heard a lot more going on in the word truth, which for them was much more unfathomable, more mysterious than merely true assertions.

In modernity most of the heavy lifting done by God and truth in antiquity was shifted to reason – and, to be sure, this was not without reason. We would not expect anything else! We wanted to stand on our own two feet, see for ourselves, and not just take any-one's word for it. Religion, in the form of the Protestant Reformation, actually played a big part in this with its emphasis on personally confronting the word of God in the Scriptures and eliminating the middleman (the priest). That was a breath of fresh air for individual freedom. It brought with it a host of changes, not least of which were respect for individual conscience and the promotion of universal literacy. Luther's Biblicism meant people had to learn to read books and that the Bible had to be translated into languages that people actually spoke. That in turn promoted the growth of a literate middle class in the countries that embraced Protestantism, which were primed for the subsequent growth of industry and commercial life, while Catholic countries put themselves at a disadvantage, always threatening to break down into a divide between a literate Latinate clergy and a predominantly illiterate laity (or else, as in France, to be torn with strife between a Catholic monarchy and the leading Enlightenment thinkers).

But all this freedom came at a cost – the cost of truth and wisdom. Reason broke loose from wisdom and, in classical terms, reason ultimately became foolish while truth lost its reach and range and allure. Reason acquired a life of its own, quite out of proportion with everything else, which was pretty much the criticism that Nietzsche made of Socrates. Nietzsche, who did not mince words, said Socratic reason was a 'monster'; that it suffered from an excessive and uncontrolled growth of one part at the expense of the whole. But what difference, we might ask, does it make if we sign off on things on the basis of rationality rather than of wisdom or truth?

The short answer is that once rationality takes over, a profound inversion takes place: truth ceases to be a claim made upon us, and becomes a claim we make on behalf of our assertions. That is, the much-vaunted 'autonomous individual' of modernity makes its first appearance, as the author of true assertions, while truth ceases to be the sun, an all-encompassing horizon in which we live, something that inspires love and desire. In modernity the faculty of reason began to function like a high court before which everything else had to appear in order to be judged rational or real as opposed to irrational or illusory or even mad. Reason judges whether claims are true or not, just like a judge would. In the place of the sun of truth in which all things bask, modernity puts forth the beam of reason that inquisitive human beings shine on things.

When that happened, the very terms that had been used to make sense of the world shifted, and words that previously meant one thing took on new meanings. Take the word 'madness', which is not far from 'folly'. It is very revealing that in the Middle Ages the 'mad' were not treated as 'irrational' but as special friends of God. There was nothing wrong with being a bit 'touched' if that meant to be 'touched' by God.

The voices the mad heard were not understood to be subjective noises inside their head but the voices of the angels whispering in their ear. That is why the mad were often consulted by kings rather than being confined or institutionalized. But in modernity, Reason established its rule by defining itself by what it *excluded* from itself, like madness, which became a pathological condition. As French philosopher Michel Foucault (1926–84) showed in his brilliant 1961 study *History of Madness* (*Histoire de la folie*), modern reason *created* 'madness' (i.e., came up with this category) and in so doing, created itself – defining itself as sane, that is, by what it was not.[5] A category (an old word that goes back to Aristotle) in this sense is one of modernity's most important inventions. Think of it as a bucket into which things can be placed and contained – like 'madness' or 'religion' or 'reason'. Previously, for example, there were Christians or Jews or Muslims, not what modernity called 'religions'. And religion, the moderns had it, turns on faith, so it is to be sharply distinguished from reason. Reason, as Foucault would point out, was endowed with the power to legislate what counts as knowledge, a phenomenon we see every time the psychiatrists define a new 'disorder', thereby creating a category that passes itself off as a bit of knowledge, hitherto unknown, which allows us to pathologize what is really just a part of life and to monitor and control behaviour in the name of science.

Truth Wars: Faith vs. Reason

The big loser in these transformative events would prove to be God, and with God the old constellation of the True, the Good and the Beautiful. I start with religion not because I want to defend religion against its critics – in general, I think, religion deserves a good deal of the grief it is given – but because I think we need a new idea of truth (and consequently of religion, to which a lot of my work is dedicated). That idea, I will argue, is found in what I am calling the postmodern sense of truth. The truth should make us free and that is what happens in postmodernity, which twists free from the overgrown and monolithic notion of Reason that grew up in modernity. Truth, I will argue, cannot be kept confined to quarters inside what the Enlightenment called Reason, not because it is identified with an infinite God, as it was before modernity, but because it bears within itself a different sort of infinity, that of endless difference and diversification. It can take root in many different times and places, in endlessly differing contexts – in literature and religion, in painting and in everyday life, in everything we say and do. It is cut to fit a world filled with airports and highways, of constant change and motion, of endless difference and variety, and it cannot be kept inside the box of 'Reason'.

So let's start by asking a very volatile and provocative question: Which religion is the true one? Raising that question is the nightmare of modernity – and of dinner-party hosts everywhere (it guarantees you will not be invited back). In fact, I am tempted to say that modernity was invented precisely to keep that question in the closet. In modernity, reason defined itself by the exclusion of faith. Once again, the distinction between faith and reason was already drawn in the Middle Ages, but in modernity it grew horns and teeth. It devolved into an opposition quite unlike anything previously known. In the high Middle Ages, religious people sought to understand their faith (*'fides quaerens intellectum'*, 'faith seeking understanding'). They wanted to give a reason for the faith that was in them, and so they sought to integrate faith and reason into the unity of wisdom. But modernists don't like mixing things together like that. So the distinction between faith and reason became a dichotomy, which presented modernity with a special problem. Religion constituted (this is also part of my line) the single greatest and most symptomatic problem modernity had to deal with, which is why, later on, Karl Marx said that the critique of religion is the model of all critique and its first order of business.

I am not saying religious wars were not always a problem, long before modernity. But the peculiarly modern problem was brought on by the low tolerance that religion showed for the new sciences – the powers that be in the Church have always had a nose for what they call trouble and everybody else calls progress – and they made every effort to suppress scientific enquiry, which lay at the heart of the Enlightenment project. That meant another kind of religious war broke out, a war over truth, and these truth wars continue to flare up in a deadly way today. Having hitherto enjoyed pride of place in the Middle Ages (and while continuing to flourish in the lives of the faithful in modernity), religion now had to face the altered conditions of modern life even as modernity had to decide what to do with religion. Religion and scientific reason squared off. Again, I am not saying this is all bad, because it means a literate laity started reading and writing and talking back to a previously iron-fisted Church and asserting its rights. All power to the Enlightenment (almost). But what I am saying is that the solution hit upon in modernity was, well, unwise. It separated religion not only from political power, which made room for modern civil liberties, but also from truth. It solved the problem of deciding *which* religion was true by saying that religion does not have to do with truth *at all*. Joining the word 'true' to 'religion', the moderns decided, is like lighting a match in a gas-filled room: it leads to trouble.

One way to put this is to say that the moderns invented the very *category* of religion in order to deal with the trouble, and set these distinctions in stone. Notice how we are suddenly speaking of 'religion' at least as much as of God, which is from the medieval point of view a bit upside down. In premodernity the word 'religion' had a relatively restricted and minor sense. For example, in the thirteenth century it mostly meant members of 'religious orders' as opposed to the laity, who were 'secular'. A priest who was not a member of a religious order was a secular priest, even if that priest were the Pope! But in modernity these words took on their current meaning, where they separated the public, worldly order from someone's private views about God.

Reason displaced truth, and truth ceased to be something to love and search for in all our comings and goings and became a property of an assertion. In modernity, the only place we would say 'God is truth' is in church; the rest of the time we would say: there are rational grounds for affirming that the proposition 'God exists' is true, which of course raises the fateful possibility that it is not true. Notice what just happened: for the first time, 'God' is on the table and up for discussion. In the thirteenth century they would have already been gathering the wood and selling tickets for your burning if you said such a thing. But in modernity, God ceases to be the ocean in which we all float, and becomes a higher entity for whose existence there may or may not be good evidence or 'sufficient reason'. You see the difference: the passion for God who is truth versus the dispassionate assertion that this proposition ('God exists') is true (or is not). Like a traveller seeking entry to a foreign country, God suddenly was asked to present his papers to

Reason. If you sneeze and I say 'God bless you', that is a sentiment and a sentence but it is not an assertion. An assertion is 'there is a God who blesses sneezers'. It is either true or false, and we need a sufficient reason for asserting it. That puts God, and the claim 'God is truth', on the spot, subject to the approval of reason, in just the way those modern democracies that retain their monarchies make the royals answerable to the constitution. I am not objecting to the latter. I am trying to identify what has happened: truth as the light in which all of life is bathed, which ultimately leads us back to God, fades into the background, and God became an entity that may or may not be (up) there (to comfort sneezers).

So Reason, as we know it, is a modern creature which was created in no small part to bring clarity and order, which it does by excluding certain things – with madness and faith at the top of its list. Modernity tends to divide things into two great columns: Reason and its other, the rational and the irrational. This is its fatal handicap, the result of which is that Reason ended up a bit mad itself, or a bit foolish, or a bit monstrous, overrunning life, displacing truth, undermining wisdom, making the idea of loving the truth look empty and sentimental. What I am saying is that the invention of Religion as a category is one of the defining moments of modernity, and a fateful undermining of truth. I will also go so far as to say that the most radical instrument of modernity, its most cunning innovation, was the invention of the category of the category itself: bucket-thinking, dividing our beliefs and practices up and setting them apart from one another with analytic clarity. Instead of the unity of the true, the good and the beautiful we saw in antiquity, the categories run in separate orders without interfering one with the other. Neat, clear, tidy, well defined, orderly, methodical, certain, unambiguous – a place for everything and everything in its place, all the trains running on time; that's modernity's ideal, and that's exactly what postmodern thinking tries to disabuse us of by raising our tolerance for a certain optimal ambiguity.

On the back of modernity's separation of truth and religion, another crucial set of categories was created to make it all work: 'public' and 'private' were rushed into service to deal with the crisis of religion. Religion, modernity said, is a private matter. This was momentous, unprecedented, world-changing, the most radical breach in the history of truth the West has ever known (this may not be an exaggeration!). It is as if the moderns reached up and pulled God down out of the sky, as if they wiped away the horizon, dried up the ocean and stopped the sun in its tracks. Religion became a matter of individual preferences, of what we do with our personal time, while its role in public life was to be carefully monitored. This had never been the case before. Richard Rorty liked to say religion was for weekends but we have to keep it out of the work week, which is what Kierkegaard (one of our postmodern prophets) was complaining about under the name of 'everyday' Christianity, which he wrote off as a sham (more on this later). Such an idea of the divine would have dumbfounded the ancients. In fact when Socrates started to raise questions about the gods, it wasn't just that the people of Athens were tired of him bothering them in the streets which got him into trouble; they also feared he was bothering Athena, the divine Protectress of Athens. His dallying with reason was taken as dallying with treason, with betraying and endangering the *polis*. In the classical world, the gods were consolidated into social life and people were consolidated into their social roles. And while the ancients may have carved out a space for the *oikos*, the household economy, they did not share our very modern public/private distinction.

This represents a triumph of the way of thinking best illustrated by Kant, to whom I will return. I am a great admirer of Kant for many reasons, but in this little treatise I am mostly going to give him a hard time. In Kant, philosophy – hitherto the passionate loving search for how to live wisely – now means the cool, critical, dispassionate discrimination of categories, of knowing how to draw borders, the art of thinking in boxes or of filling buckets. Kant wants to see all the trains on the right track and on time. Or, to switch metaphors again, in Kant, philosophers are a bit like librarians: if you want to know something, go upstairs to the section labelled Science. If you want to know how to behave, that's morals, and they're downstairs, right beside the coffee shop, where you should look for the severe-looking fellow sitting under the sign saying Ethics, which covers what we have to do (pure duty). Ethics does not proceed from knowledge (science) but from a purely binding law, which is something like a blind command. If you're looking for some time out, that's art, on the third floor; it is to be pursued for its own formal pleasures, and is not to be confused with science or ethics. Religion, Kant said, is found in the Ethics section; Religion is simply a matter of doing what we have to do anyway (our moral duty), but doing it this time as if our duty were the will of God, which we are free to believe, if we like, while the rest of religion (rites, doctrines, etc.) is just superstition. It did not take divine foreknowledge to see the writing on the wall for God and religion after Kant; sooner or later someone was going to come along and announce that 'God is dead'.

It is with Kant, as much as we contemporary philosophers owe him, which is considerable, that we start to see reason grow a little mad, a little foolish, maybe a little monstrous, which was Nietzsche's complaint. The distinctions Kant made were so razor sharp that he found himself puzzling over what to do with people who liked to do what they ought to do. Teachers who love teaching, nurses who love nursing, or people who serve their neighbour's needs because they love their neighbour presented him with a dilemma. That is all very nice, very beautiful, Kant concluded, but beauty belongs in another bucket than duty. Kant represents the brilliance of bucket-thinking at its best (or worst). This overgrown faculty of categorization is pretty much what philosophers mean by modernity, and what modernity means by philosophy: the critical delineation of separate regions, with philosophy policing the borders.

The Eclipse of Truth

In modernity, truth was not eliminated, of course, but eclipsed, truncated, cut down to fit the size of reason. Instead of reason as a moment in the life of truth, truth was measured by the standards of reason, and the fly in the soup was God. Historically, the idea that there is only one true religion and one true God has spelled a huge amount of trouble, since the difference of opinion about which religion or god is *the* true one has led to the spilling of a lot of blood. So in modernity religion is treated as a matter of opinion, a private matter, which is to be kept out of public affairs and dinner parties. Now the point I want to raise is this: that solution may be practical, polite and political, but it is not philosophical. The public order (reason) behaves like a court that declines to hear the case. It kicks the bucket of religion down the road. It refuses to rule on the 'truth' of religion. In matters of religion, modernity is like a politician whose lips are moving but who is not answering the question.

Modernity has put the prize of peace and calm before truth. This is a centrepiece of modern democratic theory, 'freedom of religion', which is right up there with 'innocent until proven guilty'. The modern nation state is secular. There is no national divinity, like Athena protecting Athens, and there is no longer a Holy Roman Empire. Again, I am not complaining! The secular state is, officially at least, a neutral public order that regulates public affairs for the common good and leaves private matters, like religion and your favourite flavour of ice cream, to autonomous individuals to decide for themselves. In principle, religion is treated with a maximum of tolerance, but this tolerance is merely polite and political. This is to say the public secular order combines a maximum of political tolerance with a minimum of epistemic respect; it grants religions the freedom to organize and express themselves while not acknowledging any truth-content in religion. When the topic of religion comes up, the emphasis falls on religious freedom, not religious truth. Religious people are freely granted the right to believe in all the supernatural forces and beings they want, however strange secular people think what they believe actually is, so long as they do not kill anybody over what they believe, try to dominate the civic or political life of non-believers who think such beliefs hallucinatory, or bring it up at dinner parties.

Without advocating a return to theocracy, I think there are problems with this solution, one of which is that the people inside the various religions, at least the core believers, have a very different self-understanding – *they* think their religion *is* true (although we are witness today to a growing number of the faithful who are sceptical from within the fold of any given religion). That's when it gets sticky – or even explosive. That's the problem called religious pluralism. It's a truth problem, and one of the most nettlesome and symptomatic problems of the day. It's tempting to say that life was simpler back in the good old days of ancient polytheism, when everybody had their own gods, which nobody would have thought to contest. The Greek gods were local, and local gods were part of the fabric of social life in the region, part of the local landscape, thoroughly embedded in the customs, values, language and geography of the local *polis*, and the source of its identity, under whose umbrella the locals huddled for protection. The ancients did not deprive religion of truth. They assumed a multiplicity of gods. So they could say that *all* religions are true, and they could have said that with a straight face then. The problem modernity is trying to deal with was set in motion by monotheism, by saying there is only one true God, which is a short step from saying, only *our* God is God. For in fact, it never fails, the one true God always turns out to be *our* God, and religious truth turns out to be a zero-sum game in which the truth of our religion comes at the cost of the falsity of other religions. This is a recipe for trouble. Cruel and imperialistic as they were, the Romans were polytheists and they allowed the Jews their local god. It was fine with the Romans that the Jews thought that they could get by with just one god, but they were perplexed that the Jews considered their one god to be the *only* one, the only *true* God. This is precisely the sort of trouble that is uniquely addressed by the postmodern approach to truth, where the recognition of difference and diversity is the first order of business, and truth has a kind of plasticity that allows it to assume multiple forms. Without meaning to, the Romans gave us the blueprint for living with religious plurality.

Nowadays, if the citizens of the contemporary western democracies are pressed on the issue of religious truth, their first response as tolerant, proper democratic people might very well be the same as the Romans', to say that all religions are true. Religion is a matter of opinion, so if your religion works for you, so be it. That's what 'true' means when it comes to religion: if it works for you. Believe in what you like, just so long as you don't get violent or bore us with it. That is also what people say about art, which is meant for weekend trips to museums and reading on the beach – that is, it is divorced from truth. Of course, if they are at all pressed about what they mean, this great show of tolerance on their part would in fact turn out to be hollow. They mean, if truth be told, that *no* religion is actually true. Truthfully, they are really just being polite or civil, trying to get along, but they didn't mean it. In truth they think there are no serious 'truth claims' in religion, just different songbooks, stories, rites and feelings; a variety of preferences and tastes, various ways to spend your Fridays, Saturdays or Sunday mornings, up to and including sleeping in and reading the *Sunday Times* instead of hauling yourself off to services. So modern pluralism is a long way from ancient polytheism, where religions were a part of national identity. In the good old days of polytheism, *all* the religions really were considered *true* because there were many gods, each a part of the local landscape, like the local mountains or streams. But the modern problem of pluralism is how to maintain the public order, how to avoid sparking another round of the Crusades, while dealing with multiple religious traditions each of which privately thinks its religion is true, in a zero-sum game of religious truth. This modern idea of religious truth is the match in the gas-filled room.

While conservative theologians make things worse by beating the tribal drums of the truth of their particular religion, there are many progressive thinkers in all the great religions who are just as concerned as the rest of us to lay these problems to rest, and they have proposed various ways forward. Karl Rahner (1904–84), one of the great progressive Roman Catholic theologians of the last century, proposed that people of other faiths are in good faith just like Christians are or are supposed to be, and so they are 'anonymous' Christians, as good as Christians, Christians without knowing it. Rahner had good intentions. He saw religion as a multi-lane highway with a lot of traffic headed for the same point, and he was perfectly prepared to be called an anonymous Buddhist by the Buddhists. But this was an ill-fated suggestion. It would be like telling women that their demands for equal rights are justified because they are 'anonymous men'. It is easy to sympathize with the problem progressive theologians have. They are trying to maximize modern democratic tolerance, but if in the interests of peace and justice and tolerance, they go too far in weakening the bit about the one true religion they end up out of a job. So they always have to keep their tolerance in check in order to show that they are still loyal to their community, while standing on their heads to recognize that other people believe other things in just as heart-felt a way as they do. They call for ecumenical dialogue, in which everybody is invited to bring their own full-bodied faith to the table. In the best spirit of hail-fellow or hail-sister-well-met, they all shake hands and eagerly point out certain overlapping agreements. The first sessions go extremely well. But by the meeting's end the non-negotiables in each position surface and they all shake hands again, have one more drink for the road, and simply agree to disagree and not to start a religious war. In the end, they end up opting for the modern political solution, too.

I think this all goes back to a faulty idea of religion, of religious truth and, ultimately, of truth itself.

2. What Do We Do with Religious Truth?

Religion, Frogs and the Disenchantment of the World

One day one of our children came home from school and announced to us that he was an atheist. I had two responses. First, I said, never tell that to your grandmother. Secondly, don't *ever* come home and tell me you are a Republican! I have always been proud of that response and it tells you something about what I mean by religion. When I say religion I mean Augustine's idea of the restless searching heart in the midst of a mysterious world, not the rites and doctrines of what are called the 'confessional' religions or even signing off on what the confessional religions call God. If you do not have religion in the sense that I mean it, then the only searching you do takes place in a shopping mall. At their best, the confessional religions embody this search. At their worst, they block it and then the only way to conduct a radically religious search in my sense is to steer clear of confessional religions. That's why I was more concerned about

Grandma's feelings than whether my son believed in a being called God. I was more concerned with whether he had compassion in his heart and a concern for the least among us than with his allegiance to any confessional creed.

I bring up religion – at the risk of clearing the room of philosophers – as a way to launch the problem I want to tackle here and in much of my work, which is that we require a new way to think about truth and to find a way to think ourselves outside the box or buckets we call modernity. One that finds a way to 'love the truth' and makes room for the 'search for wisdom' without engaging in a headlong retreat into nostalgia for the premodern world, but which also realizes that premodernity communicates in an important way with postmodernity. We need to recover something of the punch the word truth has lost, but to do this without losing all the progress made by modernity, which has become a bit punch-drunk with reason. We have to be good at juggling, to keep a lot of balls in the air, both the old and the new, the true and the good and the beautiful, faith and reason, all together. That reflects the original sense of the word 'postmodern' – a term that was first used in architecture where it denoted a blending of harsh modernist lines with other and older styles, like a building of glass and steel that evokes the lines of a Gothic cathedral.

I consider religious truth a touchstone issue. My

own work as a professional philosopher is centred on the study of religion in the postmodern condition, where I argue that by criticizing the excessive rationalism of modernity, postmodernity has created an opening for what has been called the 'return of religion'. *But* I also argue that the religion that does return ought to be a good deal more open than the Inquisition or biblical inerrantism, so that postmodern theory cannot be used as an excuse to retreat to the safe confines of traditional religious faith or as a theoretical back-up for sectarian strife, which is Žižek's complaint with it. In this book I am proposing that we should watch what happens in and to religion the way ecologists worry about the fate of frogs whose dwindling numbers tip us off to some wider phenomenon occurring throughout the ecosystem. So, with all due respect to my religious friends, I think of religion as my frogs. Every time a serious question about truth arises, the clue to seeing what is going on is to look at what is being said about religion.

One big reason an expression like 'loving the truth' today sounds like empty rhetoric is tied up in the fact that we have evacuated truth from religion. If we can get a fix on both the advantages and drawbacks of the way the moderns treat and mistreat religion, we will have an angle on the whole problem posed by modernity and the circumscribed and truncated fate of wisdom in the modern world. Interestingly, religion is a hybrid phenomenon, in which elements of knowledge (the true), ethics (the good) and art (the beautiful) converge, in which all three components of wisdom are fused in one composite, which explains why it provides a clue to what is going on in the broader culture. I am arguing that what we say about religion is repeated in other areas like art and ethics, in everything that goes to make up our wider conception of life. My hypothesis is that religion is a clue to the travels and travails of truth, not the truth of assertions,[6] but truth as a thing to love, to live and to die for, as Kierkegaard put it.

I am trying to stage a comeback for the old idea of truth and wisdom but now wearing a postmodern hat. The challenge is finding a postmodern counterpart to the role played by truth and wisdom in classical times that is not going to drag us under the waves of the divine right of kings and the old menace of theocracy. We cannot become premodern and we do not even want to be. Nobody wants to give up freedom of speech, of assembly, of religion, and I, for one, am not giving up air-conditioning. But the modern solution of tolerance to the problem of religious truth is phoney, contrived, an artifice, a tissue of abstractions and formal distinctions that come apart as soon as you pay a visit to the real world. I am saying this not primarily because I think modernity is hurtful to confessional religion, which as often as not deserves what it gets from modernity, but because without some counterpart to religious truth in the postmodern world, without what I am going to call a 'repetition' of religion, resulting in a 'religion without religion', we are hurting ourselves. The solution they came up with in modernity needs a postmodern fix, one that allows truth to move about in a multiplicity of contexts and conditions without being confined to a single method or monitored by a single overarching Truth.

Modernity is trying to sell us a bill of goods; it has truncated our sense of truth and warped our sense of wisdom. Religion (like art and ethics and quite a few other things as well) is *not* merely a private, (implicitly) irrational set of crazy ideas that have somehow found a way to nest inside the heads of certain people. Well, maybe 'religion' is all these things, that is, what has been constructed as religion in and by modernity, but not what is really going on *in* religion, which is what I want to get at (the loving search, the restless heart). Religious concerns are close to our heart – or else we are robots. It's as serious as that – religion or robots! The most interesting thing to me about *Battlestar Galactica* is that the robots *do* have religion; in fact, they're monotheists. In that TV series, monotheism is robotic; polytheism is human (evidently a postmodern humanity with a taste for the polymorphic). When I say robots, I mean modernity promotes an image of our lives as if truth were a matter of reason, and as if reason were a matter of disembodied intelligences passing dispassionate judgement about gradually accumulating heaps of facts, and everything else is just a subjective buzz. So add robots to our inventory of complaints about modernity. If we take a closer look at religious truth, we will come up with a more fluid and ambient idea of truth – one that will *also* allow for a reasonable idea of reason and science. I want to take the Enlightenment idea of Reason down a peg, remove the capital letter and put it in the plural (reasons), which disables the robots and makes room for religion, ethics, art and everything else that matters to our contemporary culture.

Max Weber (1864–1920), the sociologist – not Max Maria von Weber (1822–81), who was one of the inventors of the modern railroad in Germany and Austria – noted this contraction or eclipse of truth in modernity under the name of 'the disenchantment of the world'.[7] He said that as we have more and more promoted the interests of reason, the world – and life along with it – has lost its magic. Our most precious values retreat into private life, leaving the public square value-free. Magic sounds like the sort of thing that could be brushed off by hard-nosed rationalists as sheer superstition, but that would be a hasty judgement. When love loses its 'magic' the love is gone. So the significance about what Weber is saying is that he was touching on this matter of our restless heart. In modernity we lose heart, our *joi de vivre*, the 'reason' we have for cherishing life, and life loses its charm. Theodor Adorno (1903–69) and Max Horkheimer (1895–1973), a couple of neo-Marxists who were influenced by Weber, spoke of the 'dialectic of Enlightenment', meaning that the more we promote pure rationality, the more irrational and 'barbaric' (add this to mad, foolish and robotic) the world becomes.[8] By rationality they meant instrumental thinking or means-end thinking. We are justified in saying or doing something only if it is an effective means to an end. It must be subjected to a cost-benefit analysis, have a pay-off, a pay-back; it must produce a result that (rationally) justifies our expenditure of time and energy. This results in a world in which everything is a means but we are increasingly at a loss to say what the end is. Nothing is sacred. Sacred does not mean clouded in incense but valued – or rather loved – for itself. We all rush madly about – all the more madly as modern systems of transportation enable us to get almost anywhere – but we cannot say where we are going. Everybody is busy; nobody knows what we're doing. It's like the old good news/bad news joke, when the captain tells the passengers that the good news is that we're making excellent time, but the bad news is we're lost. That is what the ancients meant by foolish, lacking in wisdom. In short, pure reason drives us mad – and the reason for that is the erosion that has taken place in our underlying sense of truth as part of a wider horizon of life.

I mention that Adorno and Horkheimer were neo-Marxists because capitalism is a perfect example of instrumental reason. Left to itself you eventually end up with Gordon Gekko saying, 'Greed is good.' Unless you have actually read Marx's 'Introduction' to *A Contribution to the Critique of Hegel's Philosophy of Right*, you might not know that just before Marx said that religion is the opium of the people, he had said that religion is the heart of a heartless world.[9] I am not denying that Marx was slamming religion as a crutch, but the rest of what he was saying is that the sighs of the oppressed, of the people on crutches, deserve to be heard, that the cruel logic of unchecked capitalist rationality – every investment should have a return – and instrumental thinking – the bottom line – produces injustice (to which Weber would add disenchantment). Marx said we should hear these sighs and answer them, not with more religion but with economic justice. But *my* question, the postmodern question, is: is there a clean distinction between religion and economics, between profits and prophets? If we have a passion for justice, is that a matter of economics or religion or bits of both (a blend of buckets)? That is why Marx is sometimes thought of as a kind of nineteenth-century messianic materialist, a kind of atheistic Jewish prophet! That's not just a good line, a clever quip. That's my point. It gets at something very important, because for the Jewish prophets, the most important name of God is 'justice', so if Karl ever came home from school and announced he was an atheist, Mama Marx needn't have worried in the least.

Repetition

I will have more to say about 'repetition' as we go along, but it is worth pointing out what I mean by this term right at the start. The history of *Hamlet*, the history of its performances, of so many interpretations of this enduring classic, is an example of repetition. A repetition arises from the underlying truth that this play bears across generations, which keeps getting replayed and re-enacted in changing times and for ever-changing audiences. That is why we started by saying that truth is on the go. It cannot be confined to a final and fixed form; it is self-transforming, in constant transit – a feature of which we are made acutely conscious by contemporary systems of transportation and information technology. So, too, Karl Marx's passion for justice is a kind of re-enactment of the prophetic passion for God that was in his bones (he was the grandson of a long line of rabbis) and that flowed from the biblical concern for the widow, the orphan and the stranger. Marx *repeats* this biblical passion in the context of a demand for economic justice, and this allows a more 'postmodern' view of Marx to take shape, one in which the lines modernity draws between economics and religion, or between theism and atheism, or between faith and reason, begin to blur. Such blurring I consider a blaze of postmodern light, the light of a *new* Enlightenment. Part of the line I take as a philosopher is that if we could first blur and then bury these distinctions, and in particular the rigidly enforced categories of theism and atheism which I think have outlived their usefulness, if we could get to be 'post-theists', we would get a lot closer to what is going on in our lives. Then we could re-establish the link between truth and passion that was extinguished in modernity. There is a sense of religious truth, of the religious passion for justice, that this famous atheist, Marx himself, respected (and repeated), and if we cut it out, we will cut out our heart, become heartless about injustice, and rob life of its passion – for justice or for anything else. Of course, we could not utterly eradicate such an elemental passion, but we could repress it, and that would be damaging enough. We'll all be Gordon Gekkos, if we are not already.

I hope it's clear by now that I am less interested in the confessional religions than in what is going on *in* religion. I'd like to think confessional religion had run its course and we could bid it adieu (*à Dieu*) – in the name of God – but it's not that simple. When I say something is 'going on *in*' something, this is a big part of what I mean by truth. The confessional religions are necessary evils, like political parties, tools that democracies or religions use to do what needs to be done while also getting in the way of what they are trying to do, thereby preventing their own event. Truth is not what happens, but something going on *in* what happens. So, to think of truth as an 'event' is to think of something that is trying to happen *in* something. Truth is the process of trying to *become*-true. The truth of democracy – to choose what is decidedly not a random example – is its *trying to become-true*, to constantly *become* democratic. The truth that is trying to become true *in* religion is the passionate search for the things we most care about, the restlessness of our heart in the midst of a mysterious world.

I am all for uttering true propositions, as many as possible. I am not arguing against the truth of propositions; I am arguing that truth cannot be confined to propositions. I am arguing that truth can happen anywhere, everywhere, including *in* religion. I don't believe in angels or devils, or in going to heaven or hell, or in the negotiations conducted between human beings and a supernatural being about eternal salvation. But I do believe that something is getting itself said *in* religious narratives, which are populated by fictive beings and are not to be judged by the standards of true assertions. Restricting truth to true assertions is, well, unnecessary, unreasonable and foolish. I think the great religious narratives are just that, narratives, but – unless we are foolish – we should know that narratives are extraordinarily important and affecting, and we should not let our affection for computer programming, smartphones and air-conditioners blind us to that. Narratives tell us something about ourselves, sometimes inspiring things, sometimes things we do not want to hear. Truth, as St Augustine said, is never neutral; it is either something we love or, when it tells us something we don't want to hear, something we hate. That is why to speak truth to power requires courage and can cost us dearly, which is a sense of truth that greatly interested Foucault.[10]

I consider demons and angels fictions, but I do not consider fiction the mortal opponent of truth. Things profoundly 'true' are said in a novel, for example, and even though we don't expect a novel or a poem to be literally true, we do know, unless we are particularly obtuse readers, that they are true with another sort of truth – and the religious Scriptures are like that. So I don't believe in demons or the resurrection of the dead in just the way that when I get to the dramatic conclusion of *Jane Eyre*, and Jane hears Mr Rochester's voice in the distance calling 'Jane, Jane', I don't believe Jane could possibly have heard that voice originating from many miles away, across the moors. I am not that foolish. Unless we know nothing about novels, and in particular about Gothic romances like this tale, in which a lot of spooky things happen, we know enough to suspend our disbelief and not concern ourselves with facts. Factual truth here plays the part of the coldness of reality over which the warmth of love triumphs. To be sure, the Gospels are neither fiction nor history in the *modern* sense. They are a proclamation, 'good news' – think of a folk song about a legendary hero – based on a historical memory of a figure to whom people pledged their troth (that is, to whom they mean to be 'true'). And here's the important bit: *the truth shows up in the pledge, in the lives of the believers*; it is not found in uttering true propositions about a corresponding real object – say, a real whale that really swallowed a real fellow named Jonah.

So you see, I am treating religion in a way calculated to unnerve some pastors (although not all, by any means, and certainly not the ones who invite me to speak to their congregations!). Religion, like art, is about life, about living well, about matters most profound, about matters of 'ultimate concern' as it was put so memorably by Paul Tillich (1886–1965), one of the great Protestant theologians of the twentieth century, a refugee from Nazi Germany who taught in the United States and led the way to a progressive rethinking of religion.[11] Religion engages our deepest convictions and most passionate beliefs about birth and death, sickness and health, children and old age, love and enmity, war and peace, mercy and compassion. That is why religious people are capable of spending their lives working on behalf of the poor or the ill, tending to the victims of AIDS in Africa, for example, and also why, on the other hand, religious people are equally capable of burning the whole place down in a rage of intolerance. Religion is irreducibly both one and the other and the only way to remove the rage is to remove the passion; but if you remove the passion you remove the religion. As long as there is religion, as long as there is passion, the chance for justice will always be accompanied by the risk of injustice. Nothing is safe. But, once we start to beat the truth out of religion, which tends to happen in modernity, we start to harden our hearts and deaden our minds. It is like dropping art and literature from the curriculum for budgetary reasons. Once we say that such deep and elemental matters have to do with a faith that is excluded from reason, a fiction that is excluded from fact, we make ourselves look foolish. We are saying that what is closest to our heart is furthest from reason.

This modern mentality is why we are witness today to a spate of religious extremism, which is violently reacting against its marginalization and deracination by modernity, reacting against the dismissal of something that is close to our heart, and we are drifting precisely in the direction of another round of the Crusades. When people wear veils over their faces or go to church on Sunday morning, they are doing something important, not because they have heard a supernatural being calling from the sky (no more than Jane actually heard Mr Rochester's calls), but because their hearts are restless for something they know not what and are not content with the world as it is. If we don't see that, we will be people watching dancers without hearing the music. When I speak of something we 'know not what' I am underlying the search for truth described by Lessing. Truth is a work in progress, and we are on a journey whose future is hidden from us, hoping against hope that the future is always better.

So the *post*modern question I pose is this: since polytheism does not appear poised to make a comeback, is there some idea of religious truth that we can defend without destroying the political solution, which is to keep the hands of the confessional religions out of the pockets of the public – without getting involved in the potentially lethal notion of *the* true religion? Further yet, is there even such a thing as religious truth or true religion? My answer is that the idea of *the* one true religion is a conceptual mistake, a misconstrual of the sort of truth religion possesses, as if the various religions are playing a game in which they have to come up with a secret word (Christ, Allah, Vishnu, etc.) to win the prize. This is a mistake comparable to looking for the one true language, or one true work of art, or to evaluating *Jane Eyre* on the basis of the physics of sound waves. But there is such a thing as religious truth, which we can see in the expression 'to pledge my troth'. In that situation, we are speaking about truth as something to do, about the truth we must make come true, the truth to which we pledge to be faithful, which nourishes a form of life. I think that without this, without a certain postmodern *repetition* of religion, without what philosopher Jacques Derrida calls a 'religion without religion', we would be the less for it. We would cut off a certain eccentric counterpart to what the ancients called wisdom. The ancients linked truth and passion, while we have unlinked them. What is true of religious truth is also true of art and politics and ethics, and a lot of other things, all of which represent postmodern scenes where truth overflows Enlightenment rationality and permits other varieties of truth to flourish.

Not only does the postmodern approach promise more amicable dinner parties, it is more philosophically satisfying than a merely political handshake to agree to disagree. We do not want to undermine the commitment of modernity to emancipate us from Church and king, from superstition and hide-bound traditionalism, and we do not want to give up modern anaesthesiology the next time we need surgery. But we do want to be more enlightened when we speak about Enlightenment, less naïve when we speak about science, and less benighted when we speak about religion, art and ethics, not to mention everyday life, and all this in the name of truth. We postmoderns distrust the buckets that modernity carries around. This distrust will get us beyond the ideal of a dispassionate state of mutual tolerance to a more sensitive appreciation of what is going on *in* the religions, the passionate searching that they embody, as well as a more sensitive appreciation of art and ethics. On my account, postmodernism also means postsecularism, where secularism is an artifice of modernity, a result of bucket-thinking. We would do a better job with truth if we started by trying to understand the religions from within instead of viewing religious people from without – as deluded people whose right to be deluded is guaranteed by the constitution. I propose a philosophical resolution of the problem that will supplement the political one, strengthen it, not weaken it, while getting beyond both an excessively rigid idea of reason as robotic and a blunted view of religion as a formally protected right that is substantively a delusion.

For all this to work I need a good example of 'repetition'. As you may suspect, I have had one up my sleeve all along.

3. Letting Truth Be: Augustine, Derrida and the Postmodern Turn

My example, for which I confess a certain fondness, illustrates what happened to truth in modernity by way of contrasting the forms that religious truth – and by my hypothesis truth in general – was capable of assuming before modernity arose and again after its grip had loosened. So, in the present chapter I imagine an unimaginable companionship, the oddest of couplings, a dialogue between St Augustine, the greatest of the 'Fathers of the Church', and the philosopher Jacques Derrida (1930–2004), who fathered a highly heretical 'religion without religion'. The lesson to be drawn from pondering this strange postmodern vignette is challenging but simple: let truth be. Why does everyone insist on telling truth what to do and how to behave? Why not let truth be what it will be? Why not concede that it is truth that leads and we who follow? Even (and especially) if that means that truth is capable of taking unforeseen twists – to the displeasure of Pure Reason, which, like a severe schoolmaster, feels compelled to put down every show of emotion or sign of disorder. When it comes to truth we must be prepared to be surprised, to let things become 'curiouser and curiouser', as Alice said, who seems to know a thing or two about the strange ways of truth.

Derrida's Repetition of Augustine

So, here I try to draw a uniquely postmodern portrait of two 'religious' figures: St Augustine, by anyone's reckoning one of the most important religious figures in western history, who lived long before the modern world, and Jacques Derrida, who is not thought to be very religious at all, and is one of postmodernism's foremost thinkers, even though he rejected this description (this category, this bucket!). These two men, separated by an abyss – Derrida was born exactly fifteen centuries to the year after Augustine died – and by a deep cultural divide, are joined by an accident of birth: the geography of their birthplace. Augustine was born in the Roman province of Numidia, modern-day Algeria, which is where Derrida happened to be born. Then, as today, the action was across the Mediterranean Sea, in the metropolis, the Big Apple, which for Augustine was the imperial world of Rome, and for Derrida, Paris. Both left behind a weeping and protective mother and boarded a ship bound for the southern shores of Europe, heading for the big time (and in the process getting themselves good and seasick). These were eventful trips, ripe with implication for the event of truth, for the truth-events with which I am here concerned.

Augustine hoped to make his career in Milan and the metropolitan centres of the Roman world, to ascend the ladder of positions in the ageing imperial system. His plans were interrupted by his conversion to Christianity, resulting in the abandonment of his imperial ambitions and his dedication to a life in the Church, where he became a bishop and arguably the decisive architect of the shape that Christian theology would finally take. His life up to his early forties, including his famous conversion, was recorded for us in his *Confessions*, one of the greatest books of religious literature the West has ever known. While the book is renowned as something of the first autobiography, it is in the strictest sense a prayer addressed to God, to 'you' (*te*), a word that appears hundreds of times in the text, a prayer to 'you, my God'. If we staged the scene of the *Confessions*, we the readers would come upon a man at prayer, whose back is to us, and we overhear his words addressed to God.

Why does Augustine bother to address these words to God at all, since an omniscient God already knows anything and everything he is going to confess? First of all, he does this in writing, which means for his readers' benefit and edification, so that we may learn something about the grace of God that has been active in his life. But it is also for Augustine's own benefit, which reveals the peculiar mode of truth a confession contains. A confession need not be the disclosure of information hitherto hidden or unknown. We might already know the truth contained in the confession perfectly well. If we know a child has done something wrong, the reason we want the child to confess is not for our instruction but for the child's, so that the child may come to grips with his actions and move on. The truth of confession is not the truth of full disclosure, but of what Augustine calls '*facere veritatem*', of truth as something to make or do. That is what his confessions are, both in the sense that by confessing, he is *making* something, making a book, producing the truth in the form of a public document that can be read by all of us, but also in the sense that he is *doing* something, namely, making a confession. Augustine is not only producing something made out of words but also doing something with his words, as the brilliant British philosopher J. L. Austin (1911–60) put it (who chanced to be lecturing at Harvard the year Derrida had a grant to study there).[12] Augustine is thereby coming to grips with his life and with God, with his life before God (*coram deo*). For him it is possible to explore his inner life only in prayer, only by standing alone before God and examining his heart in the light of God, from whom nothing is hidden.

When later on Kierkegaard would say, 'so much God, so much self', he was repeating the lesson we learn from Augustine's *Confessions*.

A confession is an example of what Austin called a 'performative', meaning, not just talking about something but doing something precisely by talking. For example, when the judge says 'guilty', he is not just describing the defendant as guilty, but pronouncing him, making him, guilty. Or when the bride and groom say 'I do', they really did; by pronouncing their vows they make the marriage happen. When I say, 'I confess that. . .' I make that truth happen. So here we run into a kind of sublunary truth that has tended to be overshadowed in the history of philosophy, the little truth that is to be made or done, as opposed to the truths that I utter in making true statements about things – as when I remark that the tree outside my window is in bloom. Austin calls this latter type of truth a 'constative' truth. In the history of Truth from Plato to Hegel, constatives gradually come to hog the stage, a process that reaches its peak in modernity. Philosophers favour truth 'claims', true assertions about things, true propositions, sentences that get things right or pick out objects in the world, as if we pass our days 'looking at' the world and reporting the results to one another. But in Austin's theory – of which there are antecedents and foreshadowings in religious discourse (and which is one of the reasons why the comparison of Augustine and Derrida is interesting) – performatives finally get a few lines on stage. With these 'happenings' of truth, we are getting close to the event of truth, to truth as something that *happens*, that is done, or made, as when Augustine makes his (book of) confessions. It might even be the case that the name of God used in a constative, as when I say, 'There is a God,' is not as important as its use in a prayer or in a sentence like 'God be with you.' So, the question Austin would have us consider is whether the name of God is the name of a being to which the word God refers, like the tree outside my window, or whether it is, as Kierkegaard says, the name of a *deed*?

Jacques Derrida was born in French colonial Algeria in a Franco-Catholic cultural world. He grew up in a suburb of Algiers and lived for a time on a street named *rue de Saint Augustin*. His family were French-speaking *pieds noirs*, hard-working middle-class Jews. His father was a sales representative for a wine maker who sometimes took his son with him on his business trips, driving around the countryside visiting merchants. Jacques was just a youngster at the outbreak of the Second World War. When he was twelve years old the Vichy government capped the enrolment of Jewish children in school, which resulted in his being expelled from his *lycée*. The order was issued in Latin, the language of Augustine and 'the Catholics', which is how the Jews referred to the dominant Franco-Algerian culture at large. He once said he had only one language and it was not his own, meaning that he was Jewish but never learned Hebrew, was born in an Arab country but never spoke Arabic or Berber, making the language he did speak, which he called 'Christian Latin French', foreign to him. He came to view his life as a kind of 'displacement', a concept central to his philosophy. He grew up in a world that was Jewish and Arab and Christian, and then, when he went to study philosophy in Paris, he gave up the practice of his Jewish religion, marrying a gentile woman, and not circumcising his sons. He was everybody and nobody, pretty much the living embodiment of truth on the go.[13]

Never before in the history of philosophy has a philosopher travelled more than Derrida, or done more work on the road, in hotels, aboard planes, encircling the globe many times over. He said he always felt welcome 'elsewhere'; that he was, as he put it, 'not identical with himself'. In fact, he spent his professional life elsewhere, travelling not like his father around the Algerian countryside but around the world. He was a philosophical jetsetter and globe-trotter whose celebrity resulted in invitations to every continent, most of which, judging from his list of publications, he seems to have accepted. (Someone once quipped Derrida never had an unpublished thought.) Nonetheless, this author of countless books said he never wrote a book, claiming that his 'books' were really just collections of papers he had been invited to give, each of which was an 'occasional' piece, written in response to an 'event'. Often enough the paper would reflect the contingent features of the geography or the name of the place where he happened to be invited.

He had a sound philosophical objection to the word 'postmodern', which he thought implied strictly divided periods of time – and of course he was right. There are multiple forms of the postmodern mistrust of modernity embedded in modernity itself, and all manner of modernisms alive and well in postmodernity. Antiquity had cynics and sceptics who contested the mainstream traditions of Plato and Aristotle, and the reason the Church kept convening councils was that challenges to its authority (what it called 'heresies') kept springing up. The premodern world was far more polymorphic than we are giving it credit for in this little book. That means that modern and postmodern are best taken as contrasting styles of thinking we could find anywhere, any time, and our use of them here is a heuristic convenience. A postmodern reading that had the time to be more fully executed would turn on itself and show how much more complicated things are; it would make a distinction between the modern and postmodern and then start worrying about whether the distinction leaks. But since this is what I *mean* by the postmodern – the distrust of clear and distinct divisions, questioning every category (even that of postmodernism itself) – we can for our expository purposes (mis)treat Derrida's life and work as an exemplary display of postmodern virtues.

Augustine and Derrida could not be more different. Augustine stands at the beginning of the history of Christian theology and European philosophy, and Derrida at a time when philosophers spoke of the death of God and even of the end of philosophy. Augustine is a Christian saint and theologian honoured as a Church Father, while Derrida is a secular, avant-garde philosopher, Jewish by birth and an atheist by the standards of the local rabbi. The differences between the two are so overwhelming that it seems foolish to try to relate them beyond the bare biographical facts; the accident of their common birthplace in the same region of North Africa, making them 'compatriots' as Derrida quips. But it is precisely out of such contingent and chance circumstances that Derrida would see the chance of the event (and that Augustine would see the chance of grace) and make of these seemingly fortuitous connections an occasion to re-enact or re-perform the *Confessions*. Taking chances, making breaks out of chance, goes to the heart of Derrida's thought which is from start to finish the thought of the 'event'.

So before I go any further, I want to comment on the word 'event' that Derrida uses. It is the most important concept in his work and one that I have found singularly useful in my own. An event (*événement*) is something 'coming' (*venir*), something 'to come' (*á-venir*). As something futural (*l'avenir*), an event is something we cannot see coming that takes us by surprise, like a letter that arrives unexpectedly in the mail with news that changes your life for ever, for better or for worse. Events cut either way; they may be the source of great jubilation or great consternation. Derrida's eye is fixed on keeping the future open lest the weight of the present close down and prevent the event of the future. His thinking springs from a hope that the future is always better, but since there are no guarantees of this, it simultaneously exposes itself to the threat that the future may be worse. So events are risky, and if we try too hard to minimize the risk, we will prevent the event.

The event is the way we reinvent our lives, or better, the way our lives are reinvented for us, since an event arises from an exposure to the future over which we have limited control. We cannot make events happen but we can make ourselves available to events. If we are too protective, we will prevent the event. While profoundly life-changing surprises happen infrequently – we could only stand so much of that! – that exposure is always there. Daily life is full of such unexpected events, sometimes very subtle, like an aside by a teacher that changes the course of a student's life. The teacher does not know this has happened and at the time neither does the student. That is the event.

When I say, as I sometimes do, that an event is not

what happens but what is going on *in* what happens, I am not trying to torment you. I am simply highlighting the fact that the event is what is simmering in the present, but is still to-come, which links us up with our guiding motif of the journey, of life as a trip whose destination is radically concealed, a venture or adventure in which we cannot see what is coming. The event is a promise/threat: the 'promise' that the present holds, which cannot be kept absolutely safe from a 'threat', since we do not know and cannot control what the future holds. The worst violence for Derrida would be to deprive a thing of its future, to close it down, to lock it inside a body of rigid rules, fixed limits and powerful dogmas – iron-clad 'truths', where truth is allowed to assume a fixed and definitive form. So Derrida advises us to hang loose, to stay open.

In his constant travel around the world Derrida was in the habit, upon arriving in an unfamiliar city, of setting out alone on a walking tour, letting himself get lost in the maze of neighbourhoods before finally finding his way back to his hotel, without asking for directions. This personal quirk was, according to his own theory of the event, a telling instance of what he was all about as a philosopher: to make oneself available for the event, to be prepared to be unprepared, to leave oneself unprepared for the unforeseeable. For Derrida the real *truth* of a thing – of a person, a book, an institution, a tradition or an unfamiliar city – lies in the surprise it is capable of visiting upon us, which he conceptualizes as a philosopher in the language of the 'to-come'. *To say that something is true is to say that it has a future, and for us to be in the truth is to be exposed to that future.* Truth for him – say the truth of 'democracy' – lies in its to-come, its promise. Democracy is always promised and under threat, always becoming true, and we are always calling for it to come true. So we can never say *this* is democracy, or *this* is true, but only that this gives promise of *becoming* true. Truth is an event which may visit us like a thief in the night (even for Derrida, who occasionally when walking about in an unfamiliar neighbourhood would get mugged). His famous word 'deconstruction' (which sounds like a demolition derby) means finding a way to keep the future of a thing open, not to demolish it. So do not weep if something you love is deconstructed. Be grateful. Deconstruction is a love of the future.

One of the questions I raise as a professional philosopher, and to which I will return at the end of this study, is, how much difference is there, then, between an event of grace (religion) and the grace of an event (deconstruction)? One of the best examples of an event that I can think of is Augustine's account of his conversion in the famous '*tolle, lege*' episode in the *Confessions*. Hearing children nearby playing a game of 'take and read', and interpreting their voices as the voice of the Lord, he opens the book that chanced to be lying on the table, Paul's *Epistle to the Romans*, at a passage that instructs him to put aside concupiscence and put on Christ Jesus (Romans 13: 13–14).[14] The rest really is history. From that galvanizing moment in his life, comparable to the moment of Paul's conversion on the road to Damascus, Augustine went on to lay out the main lines of what we today call Christianity, delineating the great doctrines of the Church – the Trinity and Original Sin – purging the Church of what he took to be heresies, and staking out the borders of a Christian state in *The City of God*.

In 1988 Derrida's mother, to whom he was very attached as a young child and to whom he sent a postcard every week from wherever he was travelling, lay dying back in Nice, where the Derrida family had migrated because of the Algerian war of independence against the French. Derrida kept a journal during this death-watch made from afar, on the road, much of it written from Santa Monica, California (the city the Spanish named after Augustine's mother) and which was the basis of a book bearing the simple name *Jacques Derrida*.[15] This book is intended to be a performance. It is a book of truth, of baring or confessing the truth. It intends to make a confession happen, not to discourse 'about' confessional truths. It tries to make an event, to make truth happen. And a very peculiar book it is. Each page is divided by a dotted line across the middle, as if the page were to be cut (-cision) along the line. Above the line is a commentary on Derrida, a writing (inscribing) on Derrida's 'corpus', the body of his work, by Geoffrey Benning-ton, a well-known British commentator and translator of his work.

The point of the commentary is to provide a comprehensive account of 'Derrida' the author (object, category, closed system); of everything that Derrida has to say in principle, without actually citing an actual sentence written by Derrida. It proposes then what Bennington calls a 'generative grammar' of Derrida, a matrix, a computer program, which could generate, produce, program or predict anything Derrida has said or ever will say, which is why Bennington entitles his commentary 'Derridabase'. Below the line is text written by Derrida which bears the name 'Circumfession' (*Circonfession*). Derrida loved neologisms; if they're felicitous, they produce events (which explains his interest in James Joyce). In this one he is fusing Augustine's 'confession' with 'circumcision', the Christian Latin French word that the Algerian Jews themselves used to speak of the Jewish rite of *bris* (*brit milah*), which is the inerasable inscription, the undeniable incision on the body, which cost so many Jews their lives during the Third Reich, the very rite he did not impose on his sons.

The two running texts represent a wager. Derrida's mother, Georgette, we are told, loved poker and stayed up late playing well into the night before he was born. Derrida down below bets he will say something that was not anticipated by the text (program) up above, which Derrida has not seen. Geoffrey, occupying the 'theological' position above, that is, the place of the omniscient God, is trying to write the program that will deprive Derrida of his future, of the event, while Derrida, down below, is trying to produce an event, a singular unforeseeable result which will take this omniscience by surprise, saying things that the 'Derridabase' could not see coming. Derrida is trying to make the truth, to take Geoffrey by surprise, to visit a disclosure upon him that Geoffrey did not see coming. Derrida succeeds in doing this by cheating at the game, by introducing hitherto private autobiographical material which Bennington could not have been expected to know or to consider relevant. Such material is traditionally considered off limits, to be merely contingent facts about the subjectivity of the author external to the objective content of 'Derrida', to the truth of his 'philosophy', and of no more importance than knowing whether or not Aristotle wore a hat. According to the traditional idea of truth, as Kierkegaard said, philosophers in the interests of achieving objectivity are supposed to 'forget' that they exist.

Among the many surprises that 'Circumfession' provides, none is more surprising than Derrida's confession that he, a well-known secularist and atheist, is in truth a religious man, a confession causing his secular admirers some confusion and consternation (both of them marks of an event) while giving his religious critics little comfort (events do not give comfort).

Constructing what we might be tempted to treat as a bit of a riff on the *Confessions*, Derrida produces an autobiographical and confessional document, right down to taking the form of a prayer he addresses to 'you' (*tu*), including even a 'you, my God', in which he confesses his 'religion, about which no one knows anything', with the result that his many readers have all along been reading him 'less and less well' – even though, he adds, he 'rightly passes for an atheist'. His mother was always afraid to ask him whether he still believed in God. Adapting Augustine's famous self-description, 'Jackie' says he too is the 'son of his mother's tears' (*filius lacrymarum istarum*). This name, Jackie, is another secret we learn in this text. In the 1930s Algerian Jews would sometimes name their children after American movie stars, and Derrida's mother named him after the American child star Jackie Coogan. 'Jacques' is only his pen-name. In French and English Jackie is also a feminine name, which is the kind of linguistic ambiguity and complexity Derrida loves and exploits and is here a way to make a little contribution to skewing the oppositional schema of an ancient patriarchy.

The text repeats the scene of the *Confessions*. The authors and confessors (Jackie/Augustine) keep a death-watch over their mothers (Georgette/Monica) who lie dying on the southern coast of Europe (Nice/ Ostia), to which these weeping women had followed the sons of their tears, who address their prayers to 'you' (God/*x*). We see the problem: to whom can Derrida be praying if he 'quite rightly passes for an atheist?' Who is the 'you' to whom the text is addressed? We are tempted at this point to say that this is a fatal flaw in the analogy Derrida is attempting. Augustine's *Confessions* are the real thing, a 'true' prayer, while Derrida's 'Circumfession' is a riff, a ruse, a counterfeit false coin, a clever avant-garde mime on a great religious classic which breaks down at this point. Augustine's prayer is serious. This is true religion. The government would recognize Augustine as belonging to a tax-exempt religious organization; Derrida would have to pay his taxes. Augustine knows to whom his prayer is directed, even while he would readily admit that his God is truly incomprehensible, infinitely beyond the scope of everything that he knows about God, and he has grounds for hope that God will hear his prayers. He prays with and from a community of faith and has recourse to the prayers that were handed down to him from the beginning of Christianity and to the words of God spoken in the Scriptures. Derrida on the other hand, off on his own, has produced nothing more than a parody, a false religion and a pseudo prayer. Or has he?

What is a prayer? Is it all weepy unctuousness, eyes cast heavenward? Or could it possibly be something serious? Is it possible without an official prayer book? More interestingly, do you have to believe in God in order to pray? And what could it possibly have to do

with truth? The answer lies in seeing that truth for
Derrida is closely aligned with his unknowing. Might
it not be possible, then, to be a confessor who does
not know to whom he is confessing and to pray to an
unknown God? Might that even be an especially acute
and prayerful prayer?

But, truthfully, what is prayer, after all? One contemporary French theologian has described it as a
'wounded word', a word sent up from a cut or
wounded heart, from the depths (*de profundis*) of
Augustine's 'restless heart', a heart full of longing
for . . . what?[16] For God, according to Augustine, who
begins his *Confessions* by saying: 'You have made us for
yourself, O Lord, and our hearts are restless and will
not rest until they rest in you.' In everything we desire,
whether our desires are noble or ignoble, we desire
God, Augustine thinks. But Derrida is deprived of
such assurances and yet he prays. Indeed, that is precisely why he prays. The very core of his prayer, and
the core of his religion, is this unknowing, which is
the wound in his heart which issues in his prayer. He
prays in a night of unknowing for the coming of
something, I know not what, praying for truth to
come true. Prayer for Derrida is too precious a thing
to surrender to theology for its exclusive use.

If Derrida shares this restless heart with Augustine,
he does not share Augustine's hope that an eternal God beyond space and time is the final destination
of our restlessness. Eternal rest to him is simply

death – *requiescat in pace*! Like Albert Camus (1913–60), another Algerian compatriot and fellow *pied noir*, whom he read in his student days back in Algeria, Derrida is something of an Augustine without God, affirming a desire for God without God, or perhaps we should say, a desire for 'God' without God. We can also add to this list of prayerful Algerian atheists his lifelong friend Hélène Cixous (1937–), one of the great French writers and feminist theorists of the day, and, like Derrida, a non-practising Jew. The important thing to observe, and this goes to the heart of a 'repetition', is that although Derrida rightly passes for an atheist, he does not dismiss the name of God, the name 'God', in which he thinks is concentrated a great deal of what we desire with a 'desire beyond desire'. He thinks the name of God is the name not of a being in the sky, but of an event. For example, with God in the Jewish and Christian Scriptures nothing is impossible. The name of God is one of the most important names in the literature of 'the impossible', of the possibility of the impossible, where 'the' impossible is not the name of a logical contradiction in terms, like a square circle, but of something that shatters our horizon of expectation, that takes us by surprise – in short, an event. Of course, nothing guarantees that this event will not be a disaster. Life, like poker, does not come with guarantees, and what is life except a tissue of events, events in which we hope – and pray – for more and better life?

So to whom could Derrida possibly be praying? Derrida's 'prayer' is sent out to multiple destinations and he has no assurances it will not be lost in the post: to Georgette, who in her deathly stupor no longer even recognizes him; to Geoffrey, up 'above' in the theological position; to himself, since death comes to us all and he cannot be sure that he will not precede Georgette in death, and because he is trying to learn how to live and die by writing this book; to us, his readers, who may profit from what he learns. *But also to God*, where the name (of) 'God' is not the name of an entity somewhere but the name of the possibility of the impossible. By saying he 'rightly passes' for an atheist, Derrida does not say that he 'is', categorically, an atheist, in part because he does not want to close down the resources contained in the name of God and so cut off its future. Any possible God for him would always be a promise, a god to come, a lure up ahead. The force of the word God for him is lodged in the possibility of the impossible things of which we dream in uttering this name. Besides, we would have to have absolute certitude about the meaning of God to declare definitively of God's non-existence. But he also does not know himself, and cannot comprehend this 'I' who is a chamber of many voices, some of which are believers and some non-believers, and which never give one another any rest. He is constituted by this lack of identity with himself and by his very restlessness – about the name of God and about everything important to him, everything he desires with a desire beyond desire – and he prefers this restlessness to the only rest he can foresee, which is death.

Should we say then, after hearing him out, that the difference between these two texts, between *Confessions* and 'Circumfession', is the difference between a true religion and a false one, a true prayer by a true believer and the ruse of a brilliant atheistic riff? That would be a mistake, a rush to judgement. The difference is not between a man who is truly praying and a man who is faking it. It is rather the difference between a man who knows to whom he prays and a man who does not; between a man who believes he has grounds for believing that his prayers will be answered, and a man who does not; a man who prays from a community and tradition, and a man who does not. It is not the difference between a true prayer and a false one but between two different prayers. Augustine has proper names for his prayers; he can name the God he invokes and name what he desires, whereas Derrida is divested of all such assurances and all such proper names. He is praying to an unknown God. Is that even possible? He does not know if there is a God to whom to pray, and does not know exactly what he prays for. But those elements which make prayer impossible do not defeat his prayer; they constitute it and make it possible. Augustine also might say something like this. Augustine has extensive recourse to non-knowing. His God is a hidden God, a *Deus absconditus*, but he says this as a form of praise, for the God to whom he knows he prays is a God whom he knows exceeds his knowledge. But Derrida is not praising anything; he *really* does not know, is steeped in a real non-knowledge, and really and *truly* does not have the truth. His truth is revealed by his prayer. *His truth is to be circum-cut from the truth, from the Truth.* As he does not know the truth, he can only *do* the truth: confess his non-knowledge and *live* in truth, live by doing the truth, in a deep and abiding faith and hope in life and the future. Derrida's faith is not defeated by the fact that he cannot offer grounds for faith in an omniscient and all-benevolent being. It is constituted by that lack, turning upon a deep faith precisely in the teeth of despair. Derrida's is a more 'despairing' faith, nourished and intensified by the threat of despair, while Augustine's is a more confident faith.

So neither confessor, neither Augustine nor Derrida, has the advantage on the claim to authenticity, to true religion or true prayer, unless you are prepared to identify religion with being a card-carrying member of a tax-exempt confessional creed. Indeed, if prayer is in truth a wounded word, a word sent up by a restless and cut heart, then – if one wanted to start yet another religious war – the case could be made that, of the two, Derrida's heart is the more wounded, more displaced and uprooted, more cut and circum-cut, which makes for an even truer prayer. It is Derrida – who does not know to whom he prays or even if there is anyone to whom to pray or any grounds for hope for an answer to his prayers – who is more lost, in more need of prayer, who is hanging on by a prayer. It is Derrida who is required to have the stronger faith, to sustain a hope against hope, and a love for life laced with death, whose work is more confessional because it is precisely circumfessional.

Admittedly, Derrida, like Hermes, is a bit of a prankster and this is a bit of a riff or a mime. Anyone who knew him knows he had the devil in his eyes. Still, 'Circumfession' is not a ruse but a 'repetition' of the *Confessions*, down to its very staging. It repeats Augustine's Christianity and the Judaism of his own childhood home and the Islam of his native land but without the dogmas and the orthodoxy. A certain religion happens here without the doctrines of a determinate confessional religion, without the institutional structures, the hierarchy, the candles, the prayer books and the church suppers. Unlike the dogmatic atheism of nineteenth- and twentieth-century materialism, it does not dismiss religion as delusional. Rather, it repeats the structures of a certain religion, a certain structural religion, by which I mean a certain faith (without a religious creed) and hope (in the promise of the future, not in going to heaven after death) and love (of more life, of what life promises, not of a supernatural being called God). Derrida 'prays' not to go to heaven but for the future, for a radical democracy and for justice, for hospitality and forgiveness. *In so doing he simultaneously secularizes religion and underlines the religious tonalities that resonate in secular values.* He allows these precious values back into the public sphere. He undermines this duality, skews the neat opposition, 'deconstructs' the distinction that modernity treats as fixed. He repeats these religious gestures but without religion's trappings. He repeats religion without religion and he repeats the modern secular order without its secularism. *That* is what I am looking for and why I pin everything in my little book of truth on this fascinating scene, which in every way is an exquisitely postmodern one. The sense of chance and contingency, the melding of categories, the resistance to dogmatic certitudes, the openness to the future, the retrieval of something ancient in a new and even shocking form, the hope and desire for something I know not what.

In a commentary on paintings of the blind held in the Louvre collection, Derrida says he feels about like a blind man for a certain faith that runs deeper than doctrinal belief. 'Circumfession' lays bare such a faith without the God of the confessional creeds. In so doing the text isolates the event that religion contains. What captures Derrida's interest is not religion in the usual sense but something going on *in* religion, in all of the religions. That is what I am calling the passion of our lives, a hope and a faith in life itself not reducible to a confessional faith or hope, although it may find shelter there, the passion of an event or cluster of events that religious traditions contain without being able to limit them, a pledge to the future, to realize the promise lodged in words of elementary power, such as justice or democracy – or truth. The confessional religions contain something uncontainable, and Derrida's repetition of religion releases that excess. Derrida exposes the passion that cuts beneath the ancient war that is waged among the various confessions so as to see in them variously concrete ways to enact a more elemental faith or prayer or hope. He exposes something that cuts beneath the war that is waged in modernity between the religious and the secular, to breach the wall erected between these categories constructed by modernity. If, as we have said, we can define modernity as the construction of the category of the 'category', Derrida's work lies in its deconstruction – not its demolition, but making it porous, showing how its buckets leak, how its borders can be transgressed. His text exposes some kind of elemental religion without confessional creeds, spawned in a night of non-knowing, a religion of the restless heart that is restless for I know not what, which underlies and undercuts the war between theism and atheism even as it makes plain the religious passion in a seemingly secular order. His text thus exposes a passion for a deeper truth that is struggling to understand itself, a faith seeking understanding that is caught up in unknowing. This truth is a matter of making and doing the truth, underlying and undercutting the futile and tiresome battles conducted on the plane of propositional truth ('there is a God', 'there is no God'). The name of God is the name of a passion, whether one rightly passes for a theist or for an atheist.

Derrida's 'atheism' is not only compatible with his 'religion'; it is the very stuff of his religion, of the desire beyond desire of his restless heart. His atheism has nothing to do with the modernist attacks on religion which declare it nonsense, superstition, delusion, devoid of truth, because he thinks there is something to religion, a truth that is happening there, that is being performed there, that is being promised there, something coming that bears repetition. There is a certain religion in us all, in what is deepest in us all, one that cuts across the neat divisions constructed by modernity between faith and reason, religion and secularism, or theism and atheism, which only serve to obscure and fence off a deeper event. Unlike traditional religion, this religion does not save us or keep us safe, because life is not safe, and the passion for truth is a passion for the riskiness of life, for the promise and the threat. He does not deny reason, but looks for a new enlightenment, in which faith is not opposed to what we call reason but a crucial ingredient in it. Like any respectable member of the French left, Derrida insists on *laïcité*, a secular separation of religion from political authority, but he does not embrace secular*ism* and dogmatic athe*ism*, which are alternate dogmas or theologies that obscure the event that is going on *in* religion. His religion lies in affirming the possibility of the impossible, embracing a hope against hope in the possibility of what is coming, of the future which is always better, not because it is better but because that is what we hope. After all, the possibility of the impossible could also be the very definition of a terrible trauma; it might mean the worst evil. That is his religion of which no one knows anything, not even his mother (who should have known better), and which he discerned in a reading of the *Confessions*. The reading is odd and eccentric, creative and original, but it is also exceptionally close and careful, proceeding as it does from a passion common to him and his compatriot, this famous Christian saint and bishop.

The restlessness of Derrida's religion is separated by an abyss from the religion of St Augustine, the bishop of Hippo, but by no less an abyss from the secular disenchantment lamented by Max Weber. His religion touches upon a more elemental condition lying beneath the binaries institutionalized by modern philosophy, one for which we lack a 'category'. A repetition crosses out an old word while still leaving it legible, according to the strange logic of 'without', and in so doing honours the link of passion and truth inscribed in the ancient word philosophy and obscured in modernity. What then can we say about 'truth' if Derrida's circumfession is a 'true' religion, however odd and heterodox? Neither confessor, neither Augustine nor Derrida, has the advantage on the claim to truth. Truth, we learn here, takes its measure from the event, from our exposure to the unknown. To be in the truth means to welcome what is coming, a truth 'to come', which is a sea of unforeseeable possibilities.

If, as I am suggesting, it is characteristic of the postmodern notion of truth to think in terms of open-ended quasi-systems in which things are not entirely programmed in advance, that is because of the event. *We stand in the truth to the extent that we stand exposed to the event, open to what we cannot see coming, putting ourselves in question and making ready for something for which we cannot be ready.*

To put it somewhat paradoxically – and this is what we have to explain next – to stand in the truth is to be exposed to the untruth, which is taken to mean the not yet true. Knowledge is never more itself than when it stands exposed to the unknown. We are never more true to ourselves than when we confess we lack the truth of who we are, than when we say we do not know who we are or what we desire (which, I think, *is* who we are). To the extent that we think we have a grip (which is what the word 'concept' means literally) on what is coming, we keep ourselves secure from the truth, protected from the unexpected. Remaining open to the truth is a risky business, like responding to an unexpected knock on the door in the night, or like a poker game played into the early hours of the morning. Seen thus, the circumfession of Derrida is more at risk, more exposed, more ready for something nameless, for something for which he cannot be ready and to that extent it stands in the truth. We are travellers all, *homo viator*, and the only journey worthy of the name is a journey with a destination unknown, where we venture out in search of something we cannot quite say, and where nothing is guaranteed. We really are lost and that is why we are on the way. Being lost is the condition of a genuine movement, of the venture and adventure which truth demands.

Towards a Postmodern Idea of Truth

Back in the 1950s Leonard Bernstein composed *West Side Story* (which played for many years on Broadway and became a contemporary classic), the musical being a rewriting and restaging of Shakespeare's *Romeo and Juliet*. This is an example of what Martin Heidegger (1889–1976) calls 'repetition'; repeating the possible rather than the actual.[17] To repeat the actual is to re-actualize, to simply make present again, to reproduce the original as closely as possible, like performing Mozart with exactly the same instruments used by an eighteenth-century orchestra. Reproduction is a good way to get started, the way an apprentice painter (or golfer) starts out by imitating a master. Reproduction is the first word but not the last, in part because it is ultimately impossible to 'go native' (we can't shed our skins and re-enter a bygone world) but also in part because it is ultimately unproductive to do so (so we do not want to). To repeat the possible, which is a true repetition, is by contrast to produce a *new* work that draws from the energies and sources, the tendencies and possibilities of the past, the underlying event of truth harboured by the past.

It is clear that in the postmodern condition the status of truth has undergone a mutation. It is no longer accorded the honour of something eternal and divine, is no longer treated as a name of God, although as proper democrats we are not about to stop particular religious communities from saying things like that if they wish. We have all seen enough of the world to know that there are many ways to be wise, many forms of life, many languages and geographies, many times and places, and many ways in which our best-laid plans go horribly awry, and so we are not about to be sold a bill of goods about Truth or Wisdom, in the singular and upper case – not if we think that truth can happen anywhere and may not happen at all. But if we cannot organize our idea of truth around God or Reason, what then? That is the role of the event, and the event requires a theory of repetition. If this wider, more open-ended sense of truth is, as I maintain, a truth that is on the go, the question we need to ask is, how does it go? How is it on the go? If truth is an event, how does an event happen? My answer is repetition.

Notice how Derrida approaches Augustine's *Confessions*. He does not try to bomb it off the face of the earth with a militant atheistic critique, nor does he foreswear his own avant-garde style or his atheism or his *laïcité* (secularity). Instead, he allows himself to be instructed by Augustine, to hear what Augustine is saying, to open himself to the event that takes place in Augustine, and then to recontextualize it, to replay and re-enact it (this goes to the heart of what a deconstruction is) in terms of his own life and world, the result of which is something quite unforeseen. Repetition is a way to recontextualize and to let truth happen. Everything has a context and, once it is written down, it can be repeated anew, *recontextualized*, given a new life, even many years later after all the original players are dead and gone. Repetition is the way the truth-event stays moving, its preferred mode of transportation. Repetition is the mode of moving forward, *repeating forward*, repeating what has been up to now but in a new way. Repetition *produces* what it repeats.

Nothing drops from the sky. Everything is a matter of reinvention. The result of a repetition is something new and creative, for which the author must assume responsibility instead of pleading that it is a classic that demands our respect. This explains the arguments that go on about the constitution in the United States. The conservatives want to stick to the intentions of the authors of the constitution as closely as possible. But ironically, the problem with conservatives is that they are not conservative enough! The founding fathers said in the eighteenth century, 'all men are created equal'. We today understand this to include African-Americans and women, not because that is what they actually meant in the eighteenth century (it isn't), but because that is what is going on *in* the statement if you take the lid (reproduction) off. So – here's my punchline – the only way to truly conserve a tradition is to be progressive. Conservativism does not conserve; it kills. I say: avoid the rashness of Enlightenment Reason while also avoiding the foolishness of wanting to return to the premodern world, where the idea of God resulted in a top-down hierarchical order. Resist nostalgia for the premodern while also resisting the thought that we have nothing to learn from antiquity. Resist modernist rationalism without undoing the good that the Enlightenment has done for us. That is fidelity to the event. That's repetition. Call it cherry picking with an eye trained on the future.

What is so fetching about the premodern conception of truth is the way it belongs to an integrated unity of thinking, doing and making, of the true, the good and the beautiful, summed up in the word 'wisdom'. *But*, and there is always a but (which is not a bad way to sum up postmodernism in a nutshell), the reason we cannot and do not want to 'reproduce' the premodern ideal is, to put it in the best light, because postmoderns are too democratic. We are too convinced that there are many ways to think, many forms of art, many forms of life. We are too conscious of difference, and the right to be different, and too cautious about imposing our particular ideal on everyone else. Ultimately, premodern harmony and unity were achieved because of a background belief that the world was a 'cosmos', a closed, eternal and unchanging order about which there was a culture-wide consensus. The job of individuals was to find their place in that order and melt into it, to make themselves commensurable with that order, not to create a break or a disruption. This went along with a powerful hierarchical system that put a lid on diversity and lent the ideal its sweep and authority. Dissidents were treated as dangerous, not as people with different views who might be on to something new. For modern democrats, dissidence is the engine of progress.

That means that our inability to be assimilated to such an ideal is not an inability; it is not a defect but a positive effect of our democratic sensibilities. Our ideal is to let many flowers bloom, to provide for dissidence and different voices, to minimize the chance that someone or something will be silenced or marginalized, to hear everyone out, and to do all this not out of mere tolerance, but on the grounds that we might learn something new. This open-endedness in a pluralistic, polyvalent rainbow sense of truth is what passes for a kind of contemporary democratic counterpart to the ancient view of truth that flourished in a more monochromatic world – that truth is a form of life, not merely the property of a proposition. Instead of a harmonious top-down system we have a more boisterous assembly with rules of order. In a more democratic and postmodern way of thinking, consensus is something of a coffee break, a provisional pause or temporary stage in a larger, ongoing discussion. Dis-sensus is not a defect. It is the basis of future developments, a sign that there are still issues that need our attention, that the discussion is not yet closed, that someone out there is still suffering or disadvantaged, that the event is still astir. Indeed, it is part and parcel of the way we think about truth that the issues are *never* closed, not as long as life goes on. How else would the progress made by women, racial and ethnic minorities, gays and lesbians have been possible? The only limit we put on this is violence, when people stop talking and start shooting. The future is always open and the democratic faith is that the future is always better, not because it always is, as a matter of fact, but because that is our faith, the faith of a postmodern.

If consensus were the gold standard of truth and

conversation, then we would all eventually shut up. The goal of conversation would then be silence, which would be an odd outcome for a species defined by its ability to speak. It represents a fundamental misunderstanding of conversation and of its advantages over a soliloquy, which is that we always have something to learn from others. The other person is always and in principle capable of surprising us, of saying something we did not expect to hear. No matter how well we know someone, we can never really be sure of what they will say next, of what they are thinking. That is why long marriages or long friendships need not be boring (although I do not deny that sometimes boring people get married). That is also why democratic assemblies can be so frustratingly contentious. The greatest threat to our way of life is not the failure to reach consensus. It is when something – such as money or power, or the power of money – can silence the voices of dissent, which distorts the conversation, stopping the dynamics of the truth-event in its tracks. The idea is not merely to tolerate difference but to affirm and invite it. When we seek diversity in the business place or school, in the legal or the medical professions, this is not 'political correctness' but a political plea to hear what someone else is thinking, to learn from someone we have not heard from before. True, this allows the flat-earthers their say, but I will deal with them below.

There is a faith afoot here. Wherever there are events there is a future, and wherever there is a future, there must be faith. Democracy is not a purely neutral, formal and procedural arrangement. Nothing is. Democracy is the stuff of a different faith cut to fit a world that has substantially changed. We do not have the same background beliefs in an ideal order, a cosmos and an eternal truth. Truth does not mean what is eternally, enduringly the same (from *dera*, the Sanskrit word for something solid, like wood) like God or Reason, but what holds up – from the Latin *durare*, to last – over a long, drawn-out and often punishing process. I am recommending that in the postmodern order we think not of cosmos but, as we said above, of what James Joyce presciently called a chaosmos, an optimal blend of order and disorder: just enough order to keep us from falling into chaos, just enough disorder to keep the system open to novel effects, innovations, reinventions. The present is a step or a stage in a larger process which is constantly open to revision. Contemporary democratic assemblies do not pass a law unless there is a way to repeal it; they do not elect public officials unless there is a way to recall them or throw them out at the next election. They do not grant power and sovereignty without coming up with as many ways as they can to divide the power among many who will serve as checks and balances on one another. The centre of power in a democracy is 'empty', not in the sense that there is no one there, but in the sense that there is no one there by divine right or by right of birth, no king or vicar who calls the shots. No one in the democratic order holds an inherited place, a seat reserved by right of birth. The future is always open. Or so it should be.

Accordingly, the postmodern view of truth is struck in terms of the event, not of God or Pure Reason. This represents a postmodern repetition of the premodern ideal of truth, but this time as decentred or eccentric, without an absolute centre, ground or foundation, without a closed cosmic order, without a top-down hierarchic structure. Contemporary wisdom is certainly nourished by truth, but by another conception of truth. Repetition operates in a more open-ended and loosely assembled quasi-system in which violence would be minimized and openness to the future maximized, in which an optimal disorder and dissidence, an optimal instability and uncertainty, would be sustained in order to keep the system open-ended and ongoing. Think of antiquity as a harmony and the postmodern as a haunting atonality. The postmodern style demands what Keats called a 'negative capability', a power, a capacity to sustain uncertainty and instability, to live with the unforeseeable and unpredictable, not as temporary evils to be eliminated at some future date, but as the positive conditions of possibility of an open-ended future, of the possibility of renewal.

Truth, Events and the Unforeseeable Future

So, if repetition is the means of transportation, and dissent is its engine, what is the sense of truth in the postmodern condition? I have contracted the postmodern idea of truth into the image of truth on the go, which goes hand in hand with the hurried pace of modern systems of communication and information, and with the sense of accelerated movement, growth and change that defines contemporary life. Now I ask about the sense of truth in truth on the go, the sense of truth that circulates throughout postmodern life. Postmodernity, as I conceive it here, embraces the idea that truth is always a process, always in the making, a forward repetition, so that truth flourishes under conditions which promote the future. The sense of truth, therefore, lies precisely in the open-endedness and availability to change, where the accent falls on novelty, on the power of the event for invention and reinvention. This goes along with the unforeseeability of the future, with the assurance that nothing is assured, that the one thing we know about the future is that we cannot see what is coming. The faith that the future is always better does not mean we subscribe to the myth of progress, that the more smartphones and smart bombs we have the smarter we will be, and the more high-definition TVs we have the more clearly we will see the world. On the contrary,

I have invoked Lyotard's famous definition of post-modernism as 'incredulity about such big stories', whether of progress or of decline.

Instead, therefore, of thinking about the truth as did Plato or Augustine, as constituting an eternal order that is there for us to fall back on or to be assimilated to, postmodern theorists think of truth as an event, as something still to be made or done, as what lies ahead, as still in the making, and hence as a promise/risk. Truth has the sense of what can happen anywhere and of what is still on the way – what is yet to be discovered in science, is yet to be invented in technology, is yet to happen in art, or what lies ahead for us in our personal, social and global life. This includes keeping the ethico-political order open, preventing a freezing over of human relations in the patterns of the past. Contemporary theorists raise questions such as the rights of women in a democratic society and, nowadays, the rights of homosexuals, and also the rights of indigenous peoples, of the other animals and even of the environment itself, and they do that because of a shift that has taken place in what is meant by truth. In postmodern life, we reserve the right to ask any question which has been inherited from Socrates and the Enlightenment, while requiring the classical virtues of courage and hope, a willingness to deal with the novel and the unpopular, with the experimental and uncertain. Having hope goes hand in hand with acknowledging that things are under threat. Threats and hope depend upon each other conceptually. We hope the threat will not be realized, but the only reason we are threatened is because we have allowed ourselves to hope in something to begin with. We realize our hope may not be underwritten by a divine warranty or pure Reason but will depend instead on us. Hope requires courage, which is why love is risky business because we expose ourselves to the threat that our love will be rejected. Hopes and fears, promises and threats, these are marks that truth is on the go. I really don't desire peace; I desire repetition.

The great critique of the limits imposed by propositional truth was launched by Heidegger, who thinks of truth as the 'dis-closedness of the world', which is perhaps the most basic theme that runs throughout all his many works.[18] Truth for him is the way the world is opened up for us, re-vealed or un-covered. Heidegger was one of the great philosophers of the hyphen, of which he made constant use. Here the idea is that truth is first of all what is veiled over or covered up, and then it breaks the grip of concealment as it emerges into, well, un-concealment. Truth emerges from un-truth. That in turns requires something of us, a readiness on our part to be exposed, to be open to what is coming, to experience something from which we would otherwise be closed off. But we need to take 'dis-closedness' in a wide sense, without privileging seeing and cognition (knowing the truth) over doing and action (doing the truth) or desire (loving the truth). The 'un-true' in Heidegger's sense is not the simple opposite of the truth, the way a false assertion is the opposite of a true one. Rather the un-true is the not-yet uncovered, the still-to-be-disclosed, the mystery that lures us on. So the untrue stretches out before us as what is still coming. Truth has the sense of the truth to come, of the becoming true of truth.

None of this is meant to deprive the present age of truth, to say that nothing at present is true – such as democracy or science. It is only meant to deprive the present of *finality*. It means that truth has only begun to happen, and that anything that we want to call truth now must come with the co-efficient of the 'to come' attached to it, the way Derrida preferred to speak not simply of democracy but of the democracy to come. So if we are committed to the truth of democracy, that means we pledge our troth to the promise of democracy, not just to the presently imperfect condition in which democracy exists here and now. The to-come is an infinitive, the most open-ended, unbounded form of the verb, and this grammatical infinity now does service for – repeats – the old metaphysical infinity of God, where it functions not as an infinite being or infinite ideal but an infinite, open-ended promise. We mean the democracy that is promised, that is demanded, that is called for, that we call for, the one that is calling to us in and by the word democracy, the call we hear getting itself said and done *in* the word democracy. Truth is the process of what is still becoming true, while we on the other hand, who are hoping truth does come true, have to do our part, have *to do* the truth.

So the postmodern sense of truth, which is very much a western and democratic sensibility, meaning, among other things, that it is happy to test itself on a global stage and to see what comes, is deeply structured by a sense of expectation about the future, by a faith that the future is always better. In explicating his view of the event, Derrida distinguishes between the 'absolute' future and the 'future present', which is a distinction that cuts across all the categories of modernity. The future present is the future we can all more or less see coming, the future we can plan and provide for, the future that will become present at some point, or so we have every reason to expect. This future is extremely important. We are duty bound to provide for the future of our children, for example, or for our retirement, and it would be irresponsible to do otherwise. Derrida was not trying to dismiss the future present, which would be foolish, but to stress that in virtue of the event there is more to the future than that. The absolute future, by contrast, is the future that we cannot see coming, the future that blindsides us, that lands on us like an absolute surprise and throws everything into question. The future is always a function of a horizon of expectation, of what

Heidegger calls our 'being-ahead' of ourselves (more hyphens). With the future present, the horizon of expectation is relatively stable, subject only to corrections or adjustments which progressively fill it in but always in ways that leave it still standing. When you work steadily at a goal such as graduating from college, there are always unexpected bumps and turns along the way. But that contrasts sharply with a life-changing experience that leads you to drop out of college and start up a new company or a rock band. The absolute future shatters our horizon of expectation; it shocks us and forces everything to reconfigure, which is what happened to St Augustine. So sometimes the future comes in a steady linear advance, filling in the missing pieces, gradually correcting and confirming the existing horizon; sometimes it lands like a meteor that knocks us out of orbit, with revolutionary force, forcing a radical revision or re-envisioning of the world, which is the mark of the event.

Allow me to give you an example that both illustrates what I mean and shows the way that religious truth has served as something of a paradigm for non-religious thinkers in the postmodern world. I refer to the surprising comeback St Paul has made among a group of neo-Marxist philosophers who are impressed by his conversion experience.[19] Paul was galvanized by the truth, by what he took to be the truth of the resurrection of Christ, which transformed his life and made him into an apostle, launching a ministry that involved torturously difficult travel across the then known world. Just imagine the resources that would have been available to a contemporary Paul – the speed with which he could have flown around the world, email, Skype, Twitter (imagine how many friends Paul would have on Facebook!). If it is true that Christ was crucified for our sins, Paul said, then it is true for everyone – male or female, freeman or slave, Greek or Jew. So truth is a revolutionary and universal force; it turns us around, the way it did to Paul (and Augustine and many others). When we think something is true, if we open ourselves to its visitation and expose ourselves to its force, we are transformed and everything is changed, or at least, we set out to change everything. I am not saying, of course, that these neo-Marxists agree with St Paul. Not for a moment! They think that Paul was deluded and that what he believed to be a truth is really just a fable. So their interests lie in a Pauline conversion but without the resurrection of Christ. They are interested in what we are calling here a repetition of St Paul as an exemplary case of the transformative power of the event of truth and of the absolute future, the one that knocks us off our horse (which is a pretty fair definition of the event and of the absolute future!).

Truth comes in the form of a mix between expectations that are confirmed and expectations that are not confirmed. If our expectations were never confirmed, life would be chaotic. When we open our front door we expect to see in the house within not a lake of fire and sulphur. But when we open our door we may find the house has been burgled, or that we have left the water running in the kitchen sink. Whether our expectations are confirmed or not, there is a certain structural exposure to an unforeseeable future that is always in place, even when things seem quite certain. Things are never guaranteed even when they seem guaranteed, so that experience is always subject, in principle, to correction. Nothing is more certain than that the sun will rise tomorrow morning – except that it does not. Eventually we realized it is not the sun that is rising but we who are rotating on the earth's axis, which occasioned the famous Revolution started by Copernicus that I will briefly discuss in the next chapter. That does not mean that before Copernicus we were all hallucinating, but that after Copernicus our common sense experiences were re-inscribed within a different framework and acquired a new meaning. The truth we say we 'have' represents a certain stability that has accumulated as a result of past experience – and sometimes very painful experiences indeed. Truth is the result of resolving previous undecidabilities and instabilities. Such stability conserves past experience and is necessary lest we have to reinvent the wheel every morning. Without it we risk chaos. But such stability is always provisional and it carries with it a risk of its own – nothing is safe, not even safety – that it will close us down to the future, to what is possible, lulling us into a kind of narcotic or sedative state, closed off to novelty, interruption, disruption, discovery, the un-covering that happens whenever truth happens.

Truth is not a state (*stasis*) but a dynamic, in which relatively stable structures are incessantly de-stabilized by a series of shocks. Sometimes the shocks – the events – are small, mild surprises that occasion minor adjustments and corrections in the course of experience, like a driver making minor or even minute corrections of the steering wheel in response to the bumps and turns in the road. But sometimes the shocks are large, total surprises, life-altering and unhorsing transformations such as St Paul's, or a phone call that transforms our lives (for better or for worse), in which our entire life is divided into before and after that phone call. Truth can be rude. Truth can hurt and we might learn to hate it. As Nietzsche said, the ability of an idea to comfort us is no criterion of its truth. In fact, postmodern thinkers are tempted to think that it is the opposite. Truth is not the stuff of an edifying homily by the reverend that gives our heart peace. Truth pierces peace and brings the sword. Truth is the shock of the unknown that breaks into our lives, the shock delivered by the hitherto concealed or hidden, and it sometimes visits itself upon us like a thief in the night. We also see an example of this in psychoanalysis, in the middle of a session with the analyst when the truth that we have hitherto managed to tuck away in our unconscious breaks loose and everything changes. Psychoanalysis turns on a truth-event. Truth is our openness or exposure to the open-endedness of the self, or of the world, a being-exposed to an unforeseeable future – or to an irrecuperable past – to something we cannot see coming, even if it is coming from the past. Truth is not confined to scholarly treatises or scientific research, but crosses over every category of life from science to art, from ethics to politics, and bleeds into the crevices of everyday life.

In times gone by, this was less of a challenge. Change was less abrupt and the velocity with which things changed was so much lower, and truth was thought of in terms of an eternal and unchanging order. Plato took the sun to be the symbol of eternal truth because its light was everlasting and inexhaustible. If, in an imaginative fast-forward to contemporary cosmology, Plato could see that the sun was burning out and was just a flicker, cosmically speaking, my guess is he would take this finding quite badly. But, it is important to add that he would also have felt quite confirmed by the idea that it was mathematics that had worked this out, and that he was right to counsel us not to trust appearances and common sense. Today we know the only difference between the sun and a match with which we light a candle (or the candle itself) is the speed with which each flares out. Moving slowly creates an illusion of permanence, which is why it took some time for us to notice the evolution of the species that Aristotle and Plato took to be eternal. But in our postmodern times the pace of change means that truth especially requires heart. Truth is above all a matter of the future – our own and that of others, of other animal life and the planet itself, of life and death themselves, which are being deeply transformed by startling and even unnerving new biotechnologies. That is why, in the final chapter of this book, I will draw attention to the most startling changes of all, to what is going on in advanced theoretical physics and information theory, which raise the unnerving prospect of the 'post-human'. While there is always a place for objectivity and disinterested judgement – everywhere from the referees in sports contests to the protocols of science and scholarly investigation – truth is ultimately not a neutral matter but a matter of the heart. We care who wins the game and we have a passion for scientific discovery.

4. The Enlightenment and Its Critics: A Short History

How did we get from Augustine to Derrida? What happened to truth in modernity to precipitate the postmodern turn? That question requires a closer look at the philosophical narrative behind this example; first, the history of philosophy from Descartes to Kant and then from Hegel to Nietzsche, which follows the fortunes of truth from the early modern period to the end of the nineteenth century. If, as we will see, all the work that had been previously done by God and truth was shifted to Reason, then the question is whether Reason is up to the task. Does the light of the Enlightenment shed sufficient light on truth, or is it like an overexposed photograph, where the light is too harsh to pick up all the different shades? This is the problem that beset the philosophers to whom we now turn.

How Reason Ended Up Looking Foolish

Nicolaus Copernicus (1473–1543)

The major event that first tipped us off that truth was not the reflection of an eternal order but something very much on the go, both figuratively and literally, was the Copernican Revolution. As we all know, in the days before modern maps and sea charts, not to mention the contemporary GPS, travellers made their way by the stars. Following your star, or having a lucky one, was not just a metaphor for mariners in those days. Like a man who devised a swift and efficient underground or airport traffic control system, Copernicus proposed a shortcut to the problem of reconciling the observed orbits of celestial bodies with the orbits predicted by Aristotle's theoretical principles, a solution so astonishingly simple compared to the old second-century system of Ptolemy that it is a wonder no one had thought of it before: he said, for *simplicity's* sake, reverse your assumptions. Assume, contrary to all common sense (not to mention divine revelation), that the earth is moving and the sun is still – a little mathematical trick if you will. Copernicus, who was a man of God and who had compassion for the mariners, also seems to have realized that this was a salty hypothesis. He was steering out into choppy theological waters with this idea, so he held back the publication of his book until after his death. When it did appear, it contained an anonymous preface – leaving everyone with the impression that Copernicus wrote the preface while in fact it was written by a friend of his, Andreas Osiander – claiming that the theory was just a mathematical shorthand, the sort of thing mathematics teachers do for their students all the time. It was not meant to challenge Divine Revelation, God, of course, being a well-known geocentrist. But even were that true, which does not seem to be the case, once a thing is written down the results achieved detach themselves from the intentions of the author, whom we say is (structurally) dead, even if he is standing right beside us, as big as life. Copernicus started a revolution that could not be contained by an anonymous preface, and even God, it would turn out, would eventually be willing to reconsider.

If ever there were an example of a truth that shattered our horizon of expectations, that defied common sense (as well as Aristotle's teachings), that utterly transformed the world, that knocked us off our horse (and helped displace horses as the principal mode of transportation), this was it. Copernicus put an unquestionable assumption in question, that the earth we stand on is at rest; he exposed us to something quite unimaginable. It is difficult to realize how utterly shocking this was. There was probably nothing surer, more obvious in all the world than that the sun rises in the morning and sets in the evening, and that we stand on *terra firma*. How can we stop believing that? Why don't we all fly off into space? Even today, even though we know better, when we watch a sunrise or a sunset we have to remind ourselves about what is moving and what is not.

René Descartes (1596–1650)

If the old idea of *terra firma* is not true, then what is? If we cannot believe that, what can we believe? Descartes made that question the basis of his philosophy. He bit the bullet and made the nemesis of doubt into his trump card. Go ahead, doubt everything you can – and eventually you run up against the indubitable. Mindful of Galileo's condemnation by the Inquisition, he hastened to assure the Catholic Church that he did not mean *real* doubt, scepticism or despairing over truth, but methodic or strategic doubt, doubting on purpose, doubting everything you could possibly doubt in search of the certain and indubitable. Certitude was a more soothing word to the ear of the Church, the very thing the Church prefers – except Descartes found it not in the Church but in his famous *cogito, ergo sum*. If I doubt, I think; and if I think, I am. From the *cogito* he proceeded to deduce the existence of God, who is the author of our nature and the guarantor that if we use our faculties properly and do not rush to judgement, we will find the truth. Truth (*veritas*) was a function of divine veracity. God, who used to be identical with truth, is now reduced to supplying a lifetime warranty on his products, but the warranty was only valid if we followed the instructions on the label and did not abuse the product. The instructions read: judge only upon matters that are clear and distinct and do not rush to judgement. So from the proof of the existence of God, Descartes proceeded to justify our belief in the existence of the physical world as an instinctual belief planted in our nature by its trustworthy author. His idea was to imitate the mathematical method, proceeding from indubitable premise to conclusion, each step sharing in the certainty of the preceding step on which it was built until he reconstructed the whole of reality – the existence of the soul, of God, and of the physical world – on a secure basis.[20]

At the same time, Descartes pointedly and prudently excluded doubting the ethical teachings of the Church. He was willing to doubt the existence of the world but not of the Jesuits by whom he was taught, whose approval he was very careful to cultivate. He was a man of science, of the new sciences, and of the old ones insofar as they could be rehabilitated and reorganized by the new ones – above all, by mathematics. But he treated ethics and religion very gingerly, leaving them in place while the state of doubt was in play, after which they would appear even more luminous than before, thereby eliciting broad smiles from the princes of the Church. He was, in effect, already distinguishing private (ethico-religious) and public (mathematical and scientific) matters. It is important to remember that people like Galileo and Descartes were good Catholics, and Copernicus was a priest! They were not trying to make war on the Church, although the Church, to its eventual regret and shame, chose to make war on them. The Church was being reactionary and repressive but it was not stupid. It has a good nose for trouble and it smelled trouble in the *Meditations*, even though Descartes proved the existence of God several times over in the space of a relatively small book. Descartes opened up a can of worms (labelled modernity). He broke a bond that seemed unbreakable, the old bond or chain of being that was the hallmark of the premodern world. Like Copernicus, he shook the intellectual world to its bones. He put God and the world into doubt – and it was too little, too late, to assure the Church that this was not *real* doubt, that it was just a method.

Descartes appreciated that there was a certain flirtation with the demon of madness in his method of pure reason, and so he tried to take some steps to contain it. He did not want anybody *really* doing this. But still he thought starting out by throwing everything into doubt was worth the mental experiment. I have tried it with my children when they were growing up, not to mention my students. Nowadays you can use *The Matrix* to illustrate the point. You need something radical like this when you are up against big bruising heavyweights like tradition and common sense, not to mention the Church telling Galileo what he was allowed to see when he looked through his telescopes. Descartes did nothing less than create the 'show me, I want to see it for myself' model for modern reason, but he took it to such lengths that it would have been considered madness in antiquity – and then again after modernity. Descartes was a thoroughly modern man – not the first one, to be sure, but a paradigmatic one. Instead of starting out with God in his heavens o'erseeing all, he began with the opposite, the entirely suspicious idea that there may be an evil demon out there using all his powers to deceive us so that every time we think something is clearly true, like $2 + 2 = 4$, this may be the evil spirit deceiving us into thinking it is true (this is the sort of thing we normally think you should see a doctor about, who will start by asking about your relationship with your mother). Descartes put our mind on the one side and the whole of reality on the other side, and he started from the inside, asking if there was anything outside, anything else 'out there'. If so, he demanded it present its papers, prove itself by the criteria of truth (that it be clear and distinct) that he was laying down. Everything had to meet the demands of this method, or else it was out of luck, out of 'reality' – up to and including God. (The princes were frowning.) God, too, had to show up in court and present his case, if he wanted to be admitted to reality. God, too, who used to be the measure of all things, now had to measure up to the criteria set forth by reason. To be sure, God passed this test with flying colours and came out *summa cum laude*, first in his class, the *causa sui*; that than which nothing more perfect could be conceived. Too little, too late. The damage had been done.

The light of the Enlightenment meant not the all-embracing premodern and pre-Copernican sun of truth under which we all basked, but the flashlight held up by reason, which, like a good detective, meticulously rooted around the inventory of our minds, sorting out what is objectively there from what is merely subjective. The eyes of the psychoanalysts fill with tears of joy: this is their Christmas morning, the birth of the framework for the modern ideas of subjectivity and madness. This is a sea change in truth: the modern distinction between subjective and objective was unknown to antiquity. The ancients thought that some things were less real than others, some things were higher and more unchanging than others, and they certainly realized that we make mistakes, but a mistake for them was more like an arrow aimed at a target that missed. For Descartes a mistake was more like a hallucination in which we confuse a subjective buzz inside our head for something real out there. We can see this in two different uses of the English word 'opinion'. When it is used to translate Plato's *doxa*, the 'world of opinion' means the people who are held under the spell of changing things in the sensible world and are unable to rise to the higher intelligible world of unchanging essences. When we use it in its contemporary sense, it means a 'personal opinion', what is inside somebody's head. 'What colour is it in your world?' we ask in jest.

Subjectivity, consciousness, psychological introspection, psychoanalysis, autobiographical ruminations – these are all distinctively modern phenomena. As we have already seen, Augustine's account of his interior life in the *Confessions*, widely hailed as the first auto-biography (directed 'in'), was actually a prayer (directed 'up'). Augustine's interior self was not a Cartesian subjectivity, not a nest of buzzing feelings and thoughts that had to be sorted out and tested for their clarity in representing the external world. Augustine's interior self was the stairway to the stars, the point of spiritual contact between the soul and God, an inner citadel in which the Most High was maximally present. 'I went out abroad looking for you, my God,' he says, 'when all the time you were home, within me.' So do not go out abroad to find the truth, go *in* so as to go 'up' to God, for truth dwells within.[21] He did not say stay home in order to ruminate over his moods and feelings. Besides, if Augustine were a modern autobiographer we would have heard a great deal more about his unnamed common-law wife of thirteen years, how it broke his heart and hers when he left her (*Confessions*, VI, 16). The *Confessions* on the other hand are very theologically driven, more theocentric than introspective, more about God than about himself, so his love gets no more than a sentence or two (which would have pleased his mother).

The real teeth in this distinction are bared when Descartes sorts out the subjective and the objective. The objective features of the physical world are its mathematically measurable properties, its geometric form, its measurable weight and velocity, matter in motion, while everything else, its qualities (colour, aroma, sounds, touch, taste), are subjective. Now the new science starts to draw blood, cutting into the world in which we all live. Now the disenchantment begins, the loss of the world that gives life its grace and flavour. Thus begins the reduction of the world we live in (let's say, the 'warm picture') to its scientific properties (the 'cold picture'). Descartes thought the human body was a machine, driven about (animated) by the soul (*anima*), a 'ghost in a machine' quipped British philosopher Gilbert Ryle (1900–1976); while other animals actually *were* machines. The distinction between human subjectivity and objective reality goes hand in hand with a rigid distinction between what Descartes called 'thinking things' (the immaterial soul) and 'extended things' (matter in motion), which is the core idea of Descartes' dualism. Here's more madness: my own body is 'outside' my 'mind', not something I (the soul) *am*, but something I *have*, something that unlike other material bodies follows my 'thinking' around, sticking to me like chewing gum stuck to my shoe.

Descartes, true to his name, was the 'cartographer' of modernity, the thinker who redrew the intellectual map. He replaced the old Platonic dualism between the upper world (unchanging, super-sensible) and the lower world (changing, sensible) with a distinctly modern dualism between mind and body that has dogged us ever since. In this corner, Idealists: those who locate the truth in the mind. In that corner, Materialists: those who locate it squarely in matter. The shooting goes on to this very day in the 'science wars', the battle between the hard sciences and the humanities; the eponymous *Two Cultures* of C. P. Snow's now classic book is its heir. But what about ethical values, which are not exactly bits of matter in motion? Does that mean they are merely subjective? Is science in the modern sense value-free, as the philosophers say? Conducted completely independent of ethical values? Does science survey the world with cold impassive mathematical intelligence in such a way as to neutralize value terms like good and evil which do not have mathematical equivalents, turning our bodies into machines? Ouch!

With the revolution in information technology today, that old menace is upon us with a new fury. Today the 'post-humanists' think we are in truth robots. Finely wired, delicately constructed, complicated and extremely sophisticated robots, but robots nonetheless; neurologically wired and genetically programmed. So once we know everything there is to know about our DNA and about how our neurons fire and about how environmental factors factor in, we will be able both to predict and to control human behaviour with good software. And that's the good news! The bad news is that *we* won't predict and control human behaviour at all, but the robots we build will do so instead – the ones that will have overtaken us around 2045, if we are to believe futurists like Ray Kurzweil.[22] Then the science wars will be conducted between us and our robot-masters (which is the scene set in *Battlestar Galactica*). Mary Shelley's *Frankenstein*, the most famous Romantic protest against modern technology, will have been a walk in the park. I am not saying Descartes is responsible for all this, or would have approved any of it, but, by introducing a sharp and rigid distinction between mind and matter, he staked out the terrain upon which these wars are waged.

Immanuel Kant (1724–1804)

Kant represents the high point of the Enlightenment, but also its low point, the point at which Reason in a precise sense goes mad, or at the least looks foolish; the point when being guided by Enlightenment reason results in a deeply divided life. Tellingly, if the word 'truth' were somehow prohibited or lost, it would take some time before Kant would even notice. Kant does not define Reason as a faculty of truth but as a faculty of 'principles'. Universality commands his respect first; truth will have to wait its turn. Nor does he even define knowledge in terms of truth but in terms of its capacity to synthesize our experiences, and so he ends up by redefining truth to fit the purposes of what he calls Reason. Kant is the first philosopher to deny that having knowledge means knowing the truth. His goal was actually the opposite: to see to it that knowledge is cut off from truth, or at least from the true world, in order to leave room for ethics.

For those of us who use the underground and modern transportation systems, it is useful to think of Kant as a kind of stationmaster – the way we thought of Copernicus as a friend of the mariners – who makes sure that we all get on the right train and that the train we board stays on track and runs on time. Who better than a German philosopher to undertake that? Kant saw the conflicts that were already flaring up between the sciences and the humanities – the difficulty of sorting out the objective and the subjective, mind and matter – and he wanted to forestall all such conflict, which he thought he could do by carefully discriminating the tracks on which each one ran. The analogy, of course, is a bit anachronistic. There were no trains in Kant's lifetime and, furthermore, Kant (as we recall) was famous for having spent his entire life in Königsberg. But he is said to have lived a life of such settled pace that one could tell the time of day by his movements (something we wish were true of our trains and planes). That predictability was of a piece with his philosophical frame of mind, which was disposed towards the regularity and uniformity of laws. If a law is really a law, it governs phenomena without exception, whether the phenomena in question concern the starry skies above or the moral law within. The mark of a law is that it is universal, necessary and without exception. The laws of physics are the same in Königsberg as in Kansas.

For Kant, a law is a law is a law. It does not matter who pronounces it, or where or when, or whether that person is wearing a hat that day. The ancients made a big deal out of the distinction between heaven and earth. But when Newton came up with the law of gravity, he said, in effect, that the movements of the heavenly bodies in the starry skies above and the movement of the apple that drops from the tree are the same kind of movement. Celestial movements and terrestrial movements are instances of the same law: physical bodies are attracted to each other directly in proportion to their mass, and indirectly in proportion to their distance from each other. A planet is just an overgrown apple. Kant shared Newton's desire to bring all phenomena under the common rule of law, to unify the heavenly and earthly, but the task he set himself was, if anything, even more ambitious than

Newton's, because he wanted to unify not just planets and apples but to make room for morals as well. To Kant, morality is as lawful as physics. There are laws of nature but there is also a moral law, and while they are both lawful, they run side by side on different tracks, and you cannot stop either train. The moral law means your personal motives in acting should be in line with the objective universal law for all humanity. This was a philosophical way of saying: ask yourself, what if everybody did that? What if everyone behaved like you? There is no clearer example of what Kant was getting at than the duty we are all under to *tell* the truth (one of truth's appearances in his work). Suppose someone lies whenever it suits their purpose, and then suppose anybody and everybody did that? (Sounds like politics!) Then nobody could believe anybody and the moral fabric of society would be torn apart.

So telling the truth is a genuinely universalizable principle. Beyond that, Kant was making a morality out of lawfulness itself, so that you should do your duty because your duty is your duty. It is not enough to do your duty; you must do it *because* it is your duty, not because you like to do it. Otherwise, Kant feared, we would end up like the politicians (my example!) who are happy to tell the truth when the truth is on their side but not when it works against their interests. These are different tracks, and so you must be careful not to board the train of personal inclination when it is the train of universal duty that you need to catch –

even if they end up at the same station! Here we can start to see a bit of the madness that springs from pure Reason.

Notice how truth is being marginalized by Kant. He is a man of the Enlightenment, a man of reason, and truth means what shines in the light of reason. But he thinks about reason in terms of formal laws and principles rather than actual content. Truth is not a matter of gaining admission to the upper world of the Good (Plato) or of being like God (Augustine). It is not a matter of any matter at all but a purely formal property of rationality, which is the very form of universality and necessity. So we should tell the truth not because truth is something good or something God wants us to do, not because it is honourable, noble or beneficial, or something we love, but because it is our duty, pure and simple. Truth is merely a formal feature of the universality of reason. Kant has comparatively little to say about truth, but the one thing he did say was big and it was an indication that for him, as for the Enlightenment generally, *truth is subordinated to reason*. Truth is eclipsed by Reason.

But Kant's love of law and order seems headed for a collision. The train of Newtonian physics cannot be stopped: nature is a deterministic system. But in a determinist world there would be no freedom because the movements of our bodies would be controlled not by our free will but by other bodies acting upon them according to the laws of physics. But if there is no freedom, there is no moral law, since we cannot be obliged or held responsible for doing or not doing what we cannot do otherwise because we have no choice. We cannot command the apple to resist its inclination to fall. But the moral law is also a train that cannot be stopped; its commands are every bit as necessary as the law of gravity. This is a train wreck waiting to happen. Nature and morality are racing right towards each other, full steam ahead.

The way Kant went about resolving this dilemma changed everything. Kant, who had followed closely and was keenly appreciative of what was going on in Newtonian science, had noticed something import- ant and distinctive about the scientific method. Scientists are not simply passive observers of nature, calmly accumulating data until a hypothesis hits them like an apple landing on their head. On the contrary, they approach natural phenomena actively, devising ingenious tests of their hypothesis against the data, and then examining the data in the light of their hypothesis to see if it holds up. Scientific insight is a function of what scientists bring to the laboratory table. Scientific work is not a matter of mere empirical observation, but of deciding what to observe, how to observe it, and how to test what one is observing so as to observe it all the more searchingly. Otherwise the data are blind, nothing more than a jumble, an unstructured, unintelligible multiplicity. Still, data must indeed be gathered, since the activity of the mind alone is not enough.

This led Kant to a revolutionary conclusion which sums up the one but very big thing he had to say about truth: truth is indeed as we have traditionally believed, and as Aristotle had first said, a matter of an agreement between the mind and reality (to say of what is, that it is, and of what is not, that it is not). But contrary to the traditional belief, Kant held that it is not a matter of making the mind conform to reality (we say 'the apple falls' because the apple falls), but of submitting reality to the work of the mind (the activity of the mind has somehow fashioned 'apple' and 'falling' and the connection between them). That is what he called *his* Copernican revolution (reversal of assumptions)! All knowledge begins with experience (something sets off our perception of, and assertion that the apple falls), but not all knowledge originates there. What Kant means can be explained as follows. Knowledge does not happen or begin until we have received input from reality, but that input is immediately and actively processed by the mind whose function is to give this input a rational order. So a jumble of sense data, in order to be received, must be ordered, one thing placed alongside and after the other in space and time, and then tied together as a causal connection – with the result that we perceive the apple to fall *because* the wind was blowing the branch of the apple tree. But how can we tell which is which, which is the input of reality and which is the doing of the mind? The clue to answering this question lies in the fact that experience is responsible for the differences, while the mind is responsible for the similarities. Experience presents us with different things at different times and in different places – apples here, planets up there. But we always carry the same mind around with us and we know for sure that no matter whatever or whenever or wherever something is presented in experience, whether it be ships or shoes or sealing wax, what we experience will be ordered in space and time by the mind, will be treated by the mind as some sort of thing and will be causally connected. That assurance (of space and time, substance, causality) is the sort of thing we carry along with us, from the start, *a priori*, in our mind, as opposed to the variety of data that come along later, *a posteriori*, from experience.

But what would the world look like without the mind's contributions? Kant gave two answers to this question, the one more unguarded than the other. The first answer was what he really wanted to say if he could get away with it, his *in vino veritas* (the truth slips out after the third glass of wine) answer, what he said 'off mike', which is that the world unfiltered by the mind's input was the 'noumenal' world, the purely intelligible world of immaterial substances known only by God. That was clearly to say too much. His more critical answer was to simply say this world was a 'thing in itself' which is unknown to us. Kant thus introduced a distinction that no one before him could have imagined – a distinction between knowledge and the 'real' or even 'true' world – and this was the direct result of his own Copernican revolution in the definition of truth. Plato had made a distinction between the true world and the apparent one, but he said knowledge was of the true world while appearances yield mere opinions or vague beliefs. But Kant said knowledge, scientific knowledge, objective knowledge, was of appearances, of phenomena that the mind itself has constructed and made agreeable to the mind, subjected to the conditions of the mind, while the true world lies outside the scope of knowledge. There's a bit more madness: the mark of 'knowledge' is that it cannot possibly be of the 'true' world.

But this was a win-win solution for Kant, a double triumph for the Stationmaster of Pure Reason. On the one hand it solved the vexing problem of how physics could come up with laws, which are necessary, yet acquire new information experimentally, which is contingent. It combined the best features of the rationalist tradition championed by Descartes and the experiential and experimental tradition insisted on by John Locke and the empiricists across the English Channel. Of course we need empirical observation to learn anything new, but we can still reach universal knowledge by ordering these empirical occurrences into a causal chain of events. Kant essentially devised a way for these two trains to run in tandem. On the other hand, this solution also represented a victory on another front, because it found a way to endorse the unbroken rule of Newtonian determinism while still safeguarding the moral law: the necessary connections established by physics have to do with the phenomenal world, while freedom and the moral law belong to the realm of 'things in themselves'. While it may be that from an aerial view these two trains (physics and ethics, determinism and freedom) appear to be on a collision path, a view from the ground shows they are running on two different levels ('phenomenal' and 'noumenal') and will pass each other by without incident.

Of course, there is no way for Kant to know that freedom actually does belong to 'things in themselves', because the definition of 'things in themselves' is that we do not know anything about them. But he cleared the way for having a certain philosophical faith in freedom and the moral law, and he summed this up in a single sentence, in which the nucleus of his entire philosophy is contained: 'I have therefore found it necessary to deny knowledge in order to make room for faith.'[23] When he says 'deny', he means to confine knowledge to appearances, to deny that knowledge gains access to ultimate reality. By 'faith' he means a philosophical faith that in the sphere of ultimate reality we have real freedom; he does not mean the faith of a confessional religion like the Prussian Lutheran Church. He has found it necessary to restrict the laws of physics to the phenomenal sphere (appearances) in order to make room for a purely rational faith in the moral law, in the sphere of things in themselves (reality). In other words, for Kant the trains that run on the rails of physics are never permitted to jump the tracks and overrun the lands of freedom.

It needs to be added, as Kant's contemporary and science-minded critics have pointed out, that Kant substantially undid the *real* Copernican Revolution. Copernicus injured our former pride in being the centre of the universe, but Kant reinstated the centrality of our mind in reality by making the mind the author of the intelligible (universal, necessary) features of reality, which led to a wave of German Idealist metaphysics. To his critics, Kant reversed a revolution and spawned a wariness about the physical sciences among continental philosophers that has lasted to this day. Similarly, while Kant was speaking of a rational and not a religious faith, his famous motto nonetheless works very well for the faithful, who can use it to keep religious faith safe from science. They recast Kant's distinction between phenomena and things in themselves into a distinction between the way the world is known by us and the way the world is known by God. As the scientists themselves will be the first to admit, they do not know everything, and these new Kantians jump into that gap. They say that the world that is known by science will always represent a finite human perspective as opposed to the way the world is known by God.

But over and above these criticisms, which I share, my own objection concerns what Kant calls pure Reason. Speaking as an academic philosopher, I would be the first to admit that Kant is fun. He has constructed an ingenious system of distinctions that is a joy to work out and teach. In the days when we used such things, you would fill up the blackboard with his 'architectonic', a magnificent conceptual architecture of categories, forms, faculties, syntheses and distinctions of level that together make up what he called the 'system of pure reason'. But the end result outside the classroom, when the students and professors had returned home that evening for dinner, is to ignore the whole thing. For, at the risk of a certain caricature, Kant depicts human life as a badly divided and alienated creature, a bit of a train wreck after all; a victim of everything that is wrong with the excess of Enlightenment reason.

Kant was willing to turn truth inside out in order to make space on the train (in first class no less) for ethics. But these ethics have no need for truth, only of a pure universal command. If there is anything in Kant that gets access to the truth, to the true world, it is ethics, but ethics knows no truth. Ethics is not a form of knowledge. Ethics is conducted in the dark; it knows nothing at all, not even the good. So what is good? The only thing that can be called good for Kant is a good will, and a good will acts out of duty, not out of the good it can do or the good that it loves. Good will does its duty but it does not do the good; it is cut off from the good or else it is not good. And if the good is why you are doing things, that is bad (nobody can accuse Kant of being a do-gooder).

We are losing heart; how about art then? Art has even less to do with truth since its formal quality as art is to set off a certain pleasant rumbling among our subjective faculties in response to the purely formal perfection of their objects, like an arabesque. As to the actual content of the work of art – as when Keats says, 'beauty is truth and truth is beauty, that is all you know on earth and all you need to know' – Kant asks us to maintain a perfect disinterest. Knowledge is cut off from the true world, ethics from the good, and the beautiful from truth and reality: a perfect assault upon the three highest things that every lover of wisdom loves, upon everything the classical world loved. The fool says in his heart, the true, the good and the beautiful have no content and should be kept apart; it is formal universality that stirs our heart. While we admire the steadfast fidelity of Kant to Königsberg, we cannot help but think he needed to get out and about more.

When he gets to religion, it gets worse.[24] He reduces religion to ethics, which is from an experiential point of view a very stingy analysis. It is like reducing an architectural work to its plumbing or electrical system. Kant and his religion remain blind in quite a literal sense to everything else that religion is, over and beyond its ethical prescriptions. The only reason religion is not ethics pure and simple for Kant is a formal fiction; you are entirely free to treat your duty as the command of God, who is something like a friend of the court in the matter of morals. But even if you treat it as a message from your fairy godmother, even if you do not believe in God or in fairy godmothers, your duty is your duty nonetheless, and you are duty-bound to do your duty solely because it is your duty, whatever other beliefs you might contingently attach to it. One can see that God is under notice here and we are not far from Nietzsche's proclamation of God's death. If that were not parsimonious enough, the ethics to which Kant reduces religion is pure duty, formal universalizability, so that Kant quite humorously finds himself puzzled over what to do when people actually like to do what they ought to do. That so-called problem would have left Aristotle first dumbfounded, then collapsed in laughter. The final consummation of this kind of bucket-thinking is found when Kant reduces love to an aesthetic superfluity. It is very nice that you love your neighbour but do not let that distract you from doing your duty.

At this point, the disengagement of Kant's pure Reason from reality, from the world in which everyone else lives, is so complete that it really does begin to look quite mad, as if he needed some time on the couch. Reading Kant's philosophy is like reading the work of an extraterrestrial being sent down to earth to make an inventory of a curious sublunary species whose heads come equipped with a intricate system of buckets, gears and gauges by means of which they make their way around a world of whose true reality they profess to know nothing, while marching in step with a voice which they profess not to understand, and which commands them to act in a world whose pleasures they carefully monitor lest they fall in love with their life.[25]

This was a very long way from what the ancients called wisdom, and a lot closer to what they considered foolish. Kant died in 1804, and a storm of criticism broke out in the nineteenth century, in which both the philosophers and the Romantic poets called for a return to the concreteness of life, to the concrete truth of life, a cause for which I would gladly write a cheque.

Hegel's Critique of the Enlightenment

After Kant, the great philosophers in whom truth stages a comeback, and certainly the most instructive for our postmodern times, are Georg Wilhelm Friedrich Hegel (1770–1831), Søren Kierkegaard (1813–55) and Friedrich Nietzsche (1844–1900). I can hear my audience snickering. If my complaint with pure Reason is that it finally leads to madness it seems no less mad a choice to turn to Hegel, Kierkegaard and Nietzsche for relief. Hegel was the subject of a merciless lampooning by Kierkegaard as the absolute professor, the man who had confused himself not with his hat but with God, as if God had come into the world in order to arrange a consultation with German metaphysics about the make-up of the divine nature. Kierkegaard on the other hand was known as the 'melancholy Dane' and led an eccentric and depressed life, while Nietzsche went certifiably mad. So there is some truth to saying that the madness to which Enlightenment reason leads is met by its counterpart, an anti-Enlightenment madness which reacts against it. But Hegel was quite a sober man who made a penetrating critique of the Enlightenment from which it never recovered, and while Kierkegaard and Nietzsche were each in their own way mad as hatters, they are like the canaries in the coal mine of modernity, and their works were exquisite lamentations over what the Enlightenment wrought. Together, albeit in different ways, these three break open the space of postmodern thought by returning us to the question of truth. True to my hypothesis, each man's position strikes a defining relation with religion, although each generates distinct problems of its own, problems that can be ironed out in the next chapter when we get to the 'postmodern turn'.

In 1806, when Hegel was a young professor in the city of Jena, French forces led by Napoleon himself occupied the city. Hegel, who was an admirer of the French Revolution, was in the crowd watching the famous man leading the march, compelling him to remark that he was observing the 'world spirit on horseback' (that was of course the only means of transportation available for world spirits at that time, later on they would have private jets). For Hegel, Napoleon was not just this mere mortal man of flesh and blood, and this was not just another horse ride, nor was this just another military march: this was the march of history, of the world spirit. By 'spirit' Hegel meant that individual people are not isolated units but parts of a larger whole, a *Zeitgeist*, the spirit of the age, an underlying force or historical energy which urges them forward. Certain individuals, like Napoleon, have caught, or been caught up in, this spirit in a special way.[26]

This observation about Napoleon on Hegel's part is not just a bit of whimsy, a personal anecdote, an attempt to add local colour or an example to an otherwise difficulty philosophy. It contains the very nub of his critique of the Enlightenment and of the way in which it had impoverished the idea of truth. Truth, Hegel said, is not accessed by bucket-thinking (I am paraphrasing!) but by a holistic sense of the 'concrete'. But by insisting upon the concrete, he is not making a pedagogical point, that if you cannot give an example you do not understand it. While that is true, Hegel is making a more fundamental philosophical point about the nature of reality and of truth, which is, we might say, that if reality cannot exemplify itself, it is not really true. I readily admit that anyone who has picked up a paperback edition of Hegel's *Logic* to read on the ride to work in the morning will greet my observation that Hegel's philosophy is 'concrete' with a smile. To be sure, his writing is fiercely cerebral and punishingly difficult to read. He often sounds like a spoof of a German philosopher in a Gilbert and Sullivan operetta. So if he calls his philosophy concrete and this does not mean that he is merciful to his readers – he most certainly is not – what does concrete mean?

Hegel is opposing Kant's very formal, analytic-discriminating approach to truth, so typical of the Enlightenment, to an organic, synthesizing way of thinking, where things are bound together from the start in a living unity and a developing whole. Hegel thus meant 'concrete' in a literal way, where the universal and the particular, the transcendent and the immanent, the eternal and the temporal, God and the world, the spirit and the individual mesh together (*con* + *crescere*), as they do in the figure of Napoleon, not merely so that we can understand the truth but in order for the truth to exist! Truth is not just an abstract name: it actually appears in history, sitting on the back of a horse. Truth is not merely a formal property of propositions reached by following the rules of method; truth is something substantial, something concrete, the substance of our lives, of history. Truth is the march of the spirit through time – which is Hegelspeak for saying that truth is realized only in and through the life of concrete individuals, peoples and ages – without which the spirit is unreal, a mere abstraction, a ghost. Incidentally, if you are wondering where the spirit came from, the answer is that while it is constantly becoming it did not originally come from anything. It is eternal, like God, which in fact is the name given to Hegel's Spirit in religion. For Hegel, what is called God in religion comes down to earth and lives in space and time and rides about on horses.

Think of the analytic method of Kant and the Enlightenment as the knowledge someone has of a city they have never visited but only read about. They have seen books of photographs in which the various parts of the city are displayed in an orderly way, each chapter devoted to a separate neighbourhood. Compare that to the knowledge people who have lived in the city all their lives have, who know the short cuts and the best restaurants, who have watched neighbourhoods change and seen the city evolve into its present form. Whereas the Kantians have an abstract, pale and piecemeal knowledge of city, Hegel thinks *truth is the whole*, the concrete unity of the whole, the way things mesh. Descartes and Kant had conceived of truth as a matter of analytically clearing one's head, as a matter of keeping human beliefs and practices compartmentalized, of following a method. Kant is like a pathologist analysing a sample under a slide whereas Hegel says it is the whole person who is ill. Kant thought of truth as an archipelago, the island of science here, of ethics there, of aesthetics in between, which requires of us the ability to island hop (note that religion does not get its own island, but is granted planning permission to construct its houses of worship on the island of ethics). But Hegel considered this to be a fundamentally mistaken frame of mind. He called it abstract, one-sided thinking, logic-chopping, thereby consigning philosophy to a futile attempt to piece things back together after they have been torn asunder. That is why we ended up with what I called the madness and alienation of life in a world of pure Reason, as when Kant found it problematic that someone might actually like to do what they were obliged to do. For Kant it was a problem to be solved that someone liked their job; for Hegel, not to like your job is to live an alienated life, a thought that Marx made a point of departure for his critique of capitalism.

Hegel launched a full-scale attack on the Enlightenment in the name of truth. No philosopher since antiquity has ever made truth more central than Hegel. He reminds us of Plato and the medieval theologians on this point, where truth is not treated only as a correspondence between a proposition and reality (propositional truth) but as the very substance of reality itself (ontological truth) and the very light of the mind (Augustine). Hegel could say that God is truth without crossing his fingers behind his back, although he would add that we need to bring in the philosophers to clear that up. But unlike Plato and the medieval theologians, for whom eternity and time, heaven and earth, being and becoming belonged to distinctly different spheres or realms, like Augustine's city of God and city of man, Hegel's idea was to unite these seemingly opposite realms and to unite them in the concrete, to think in terms of a larger picture of being-*in*-becoming, eternity-*in*-time, transcendence-*in*-immanence, heaven-*on*-earth, God-*in*-the-world, where to separate one from the other was to fall into abstract thinking. Truth is not found on just one side of an opposition but in a unity of opposites. Truth is not an abstraction. It is the very process of concretizing itself, exemplifying itself, realizing itself. Truth is a march, in motion, coming about or coming to be in space and time, absent from which it is not real at all. Everything that is real is in equal measure true, and everything that is true is in equal measure real, a stage of truth's concrete development in the physical world. With Hegel, we finally meet a philosopher who says that truth is a thing of this world, that truth is the process of becoming-true, that truth can happen anywhere. Finally, someone says that truth is on the go. While he certainly did not foresee the dizzying pace of the lives we lead today, his whole idea was that reality is ongoing, an incessant process that never attains a fixed form.

The Origin of Species did not appear until 1859, almost thirty years after Hegel's death, but he would have bought several copies. Hegel thought that history was restricted to our cultural life, but the idea that nature also has a history was a perfect fit for his metaphysics, where historical development is all. Hegel would have welcomed Darwin's notion that fish and birds and human beings are not simply different static species, marked off or discriminated from each other by unchanging species-specific traits, but varying stages of the evolution of life on earth, and that the human body bears the marks of having passed through all these stages, in just the way those who have spent their whole lives in a city can still see traces of the old neighbourhoods and point out old landmarks. Hegel, like Napoleon, travelled on horseback and did not live to see the Industrial Revolution, or to see how much we would learn about natural history. But he is the first great philosopher to make history a philosophical problem, to analyse where it was going, and to say its development is an intrinsic part of the way truth itself, like Darwin's species, has developed into its current form. He was the first one to recognize that to understand truth is to understand where and how things are on the move.

When Hegel speaks of the underlying substance of reality as the 'spirit' (*Geist*), let us say for the sake of clarification a 'spiral'. Spirit/spiral is a play on words in English, but it does do some work for us. A spiral circles around and around, not in a flat or unproductive repetition but in a steady ascent, circling over itself, higher and higher until it comes to a head, a peak or pinnacle, where it has finally become itself, has come into its truth. We might be tempted to say that at the peak or pinnacle we reach 'the end of history'. The fall of the Iron Curtain in 1989 prompted Francis Fukuyama to proclaim that we had actually reached the end of history, by which he meant the victory of Reagan-Thatcherite free market capitalism. That euphoria was a bit of badly misguided and amusing right-wing Hegelianism. Hegel did not think history closed at this point, or at any other point. In the same way that it did not come from anywhere, it was not going to go away. That is what he meant when he called the world spirit 'eternal', which did not mean outside time but rather infinite, unending time. When the spirit/spiral reaches its highest stage of development that stage is itself the beginning of a new and higher spiral, and the spirals just keep spiralling, reaching ever-higher and more refined points for ever, infinitesimally approaching infinity. This high point for him is measured not by the size of your stock portfolio, *pace* Fukuyama, but by knowledge. The very nature of things is becoming-true, spirit spiralling into truth, in which spirit spreads its wings and ascends in successively upward circles in the process of developing or becoming what it is, what it truly is, what it is in truth, the way the acorn becomes an oak or the infant becomes an adult.

It is important to see that spirit or truth is not a 'somebody' who does things. That is what Slavoj Žižek calls a 'scarecrow Hegel', as if the spirit were a cunning super-individual who manipulates the rest of us more benighted individuals down below. Hegel realized perfectly well that we human beings are the only agents, the only ones who do things, but he was saying that we are not isolated autonomous agents. Napoleon is not an island, although he ended up on one. He embodies the spirit of the age and is prompted by it, but the spirit is not a super-somebody working Napoleon like a puppet. What we do is the unfolding life, the realization, of the spirit of the age or of history in and through us. Without us, the spirit is nothing real. Without the spirit, we are uninspired and have nothing to realize. So we belong together 'concretely'.

We can see what Hegel is up to when we see what he is doing to and with religion. If Napoleon is a concrete figure in which the aspirations of the spirit were focused, Jesus Christ is even more so. It is no exaggeration to say that Hegel's entire philosophy is an unorthodox rendering (repetition) of the Incarnation. Hegel had both good news and bad news for Christianity. The good news is that it is the absolute truth, to which the Lutheran Church of his day nodded in pious approval. The bad news is that it is the absolute truth in figurative form. The 'figurative' bit made the Church lurch forward in its seat. Religion presents the truth in stories about God 'above' and the world 'below', and of God coming down to earth, being born in a manger while angels sang in the background, dying for our sins and ascending into heaven, and leaving behind his 'spirit'(!). Hegel said that this is all true, the absolute truth, the truth about the absolute – in the form of a *story*. But the task remains to interpret and understand this story. That is when we have to call in the philosophers for a consultation. Circling over religion like an eagle (that's Derrida making a French pun, Hegel/*aigle*), the philosophers swoop down upon the images and figures in religion and restate them with conceptual accuracy, in their truth: what we call God in religion is, truth to tell, what Hegel, back in the philosophy department, called the 'absolute spirit'. The Christian story they tell in the churches is rendered more precisely in the philosophy department. It is really telling us that God's true nature is to unfold in space and time and that the old transcendent God up in the sky is an imaginative way of speaking. It is, for example, hopelessly pre-Copernican. After Copernicus, 'up' has lost its punch; 'up' is out. This declaration was not greeted warmly by the Church hierarchy, and they denounced it as pantheism! Technically it is not pantheism, but what was later on called 'pan*en*theism', God-in-all, all-in-God, that is, the *concrete* unity of God-in-the-world and the world-in-God, the two together. God is not identical with you, your grandmother or Hegel, or with any particular entity at all – *that's* pantheism – but God is the enduring infinite substance in which particular finite entities come and go, in which and through which God's life is realized. Without the world, God has no reality; without God, the world has nothing to realize. The human community realizes God's life on earth, actualizing the spirit that is 'figured' by Jesus ascending into heaven and leaving the Holy Spirit behind.

For Hegel, religion is an important clue to what is going on with truth. He represents the first version of the *repetition* of religion that I described in Derrida's reading of Augustine, where the right way to approach religion is not simply to critique it but to repeat it. He does not attempt the sort of ham-fisted hammering of religious superstition typified by the old-fashioned Enlightenment atheism. We should remember that while the efforts of the early Enlightenment rationalists like Descartes and others were directed at coming up with rational proofs for the existence of God, the tide would eventually turn in the nineteenth century. The evidence for scientific naturalism and 'atheism' – the term first acquires currency in France in the eighteenth century – began to mount up, making God look like an unnecessary hypothesis and leading to the contemporary theological impasse of bringing in God at the last minute to close up a gap. The writing was on the wall about a God such as that. The battle between rational theology and rationalist atheism was first engaged in earnest then and, unhappily, continues to this day. Hegel will have none of this. Instead Hegel thinks there is something going on *in* religion that demands our reflection and attention, which for Hegel meant that it is up to the philosophers to discern what form the spirit is taking in religion, which requires reading it from within (to catch its spirit). Whatever happens for Hegel, whatever is in any way real – be it science, ethics, politics, art or religion – embodies some form of the truth, some stage in its development, and the work of philosophy is to work this out, to feel about for the particular shape truth has taken in any particular figure of the spirit, whatever its form. If it did not, it would not be there; it would not be real. By the way, if you are wondering how we are supposed to tell who counts and who does not as a world historical figure, the answer is it is one part seat of your pants and one part your seat in the library. That is, you sift through an enormous amount of historical information – and Hegel did that – until you 'catch' (intuit) the spirit of the age at work in a historical event, a paradigmatic work of art or a religious practice, and then tell the story of the age that turns on that focal object in a convincing way.

But you can do all this only after the fact, at the end of the age, looking back. The owl of Minerva, he said, only spreads its wings at dusk.

But while my hat is off to Hegel's work as a breakthrough which undertakes a repetition of religion instead of engaging either in futile rationalist proofs of the existence of God and the immortality of the soul, or in rationalist refutations of religion, his repetition is too much of a good thing. It is far too powerful; it goes too far. Religion undergoes a meltdown when exposed to the high heat of Hegel's All-Grasping *Begriff* ('concept', literally a 'grasping'), when it is seized by the claws of the Hegel/*aigle*. The difference between Hegel's and Derrida's repetition of religion is that Derrida leaves us in a deep non-knowing, a prayerful openness to and faith in an unforeseeable future, which is the structure of truth for Derrida. Derrida always worries about making our idea of truth too strong, about people who claim to have *the* truth. That is why Gianni Vattimo (1936–), an Italian postmodern thinker, writes in praise of 'weak thought' as opposed to traditional metaphysical thinking, which is too strong (or dogmatic). For example, Kierkegaard – who was inspired by Lessing's thesis – would defer the compliment that he *is* a Christian in favour of saying he is trying to *become* one. Derrida would add that in trying to become a *Christian*, or anything else, Kierkegaard does not truly know *what* he is trying to become. We do not know what we desire and that is the condition under which a more radical desire is possible, so that for Derrida we are all, Augustine and Kierkegaard and everyone else alike, afloat or adrift in the same boat, a boat whose final destination neither Hegel nor anyone else knows. Compared to Derrida, Hegel is a bit of a know-it-all, someone who thinks that the philosophers arrive on the scene at the crucial point to explain everything – like a detective at the end of a novel – and unravel the deepest structures of truth to everyone else who knew that something important was going on but couldn't figure out what.

So for all the criticism he directed at the Enlightenment, Hegel remained in the grip of the deepest assumption of the Enlightenment, which is that the world is indeed a system of reason – so long as reason is understood concretely. There is nothing about reality to which reason is denied access. The postmodern view, on the other hand, is that this is a bit of overreaching, that truth is on the go but we are not sure where it is going or whether it is just one unified thing, and we reserve our opinion about what is finally going on. Philosophers like Heidegger and Derrida think that history is something of a roll of the dice, that nothing is guaranteed, that truth might remain for ever concealed and things might turn out badly. Hegel, on the other hand, thought history was all a sure thing, underwritten by the Spirit – which we might think of as a great German insurance company with infinite resources to underwrite all disasters and keep everything on course. (Sounds like what the European Union wants today.) But postmoderns strongly doubt, after the genocides of the twentieth century, that history is the unfolding of God's life on earth, which would get us back into the old problem of theodicy, of finding a way to say that the worst evils are just part of God's infinite but mysterious plan. To look for the divine love behind the Holocaust is, as Lyotard said, an obscenity. Had Hegel lived through the twentieth century, we have to think he might have rethought his position.

We can also see what goes wrong in Hegel if we pressed him for a concrete example of absolute truth. Hegel would have replied that, with all due modesty, the constitutional monarchy of the Prussia of his day, and especially the University of Berlin, and, now that he thinks about it, the philosophy department in particular, were pretty much the summit of God's life on earth. That was the sort of thing that sent Kierkegaard into spasms of ridicule. That was surely mad! It was at least not a very good example of the kind of eccentric wisdom I am trying to conjure up for our postmodern times, which turns on a plurality of little truths. With Hegel, then, we reach a kind of consummation of what the Greeks first called philosophy, but one that flies too close to the sun. While the Greeks started it all by calling philosophy a loving search for truth, Hegel sometimes sounded like he was calling off the search, declaring he had found it, which brings us back yet again to Lessing's thesis about choosing the left hand of God, which befits mere mortals searching for the truth, instead of trying to occupy a God's-eye view and claiming to have the truth.

Hegel set off a torrent of anti-philosophy, or post-philosophy, in which philosophers philosophize against Hegel and the tremendous reach that philosophy had grasped for in Hegel. His successors react against him in various ways – by being more materialist than idealist (Marx), more interested in the existential individual than in world history (Kierkegaard), and more atheistic than panentheistic (Nietzsche). They all proposed different candidates for what is truly concrete, but they did not dispute that concrete is what truth is and must be. So, there was more work to do. Kierkegaard would insist that the genuine concrete truth is the concretely 'existing' individual who stands alone before God, while for Nietzsche, the truly concrete individual affirms a godless love of the earth and time and bodily life, where 'truthfulness' lies in not succumbing to the illusory supernatural truth Christianity and Platonism perpetuate. I will show below how Hegel, Kierkegaard and Nietzsche each contribute something crucial to the eventual postmodern turn taken by truth today.

5. Postmodern Prophets

Kierkegaard and Nietzsche are the closest thing we have to modern, or rather postmodern, prophets. They made uncannily accurate calls about what was becoming of us in modernity and focused their critique on the corruption and decadence truth had undergone in modern times. This was a first, an odd observation for a philosopher to make – to consider the corrosive effects of the surrounding culture. What we today call 'cultural studies' is in their debt, and in Hegel's too. Hitherto the philosophers thought reflecting upon truth a purely academic and intellectual exercise. But Kierkegaard and Nietzsche think that what philosophers had been in the habit of calling truth is something of an intellectual fiction, an armchair construction, bred in an academic hothouse rather than grown in the wild of the real world. Truth for them, on the other hand, is something that is deeply disturbing, filling us personally with 'fear and trembling' (Kierkegaard), and sending us back to Greek tragedy (Nietzsche) – as opposed to the frail and malnourished weakling that perishes almost instantly upon making contact with the air outside the academy. Truth is a matter of blood, sweat and tears, something visited upon us in an unguarded moment, forcing us to stare into the abyss. They mock the chalk-dust definitions of truth drawn up by the pale philosophers, the 'last fumes of evaporating reality', as Nietzsche called them.[27] So Nietzsche slammed the door of the university behind him and began a life of wandering, of free thinking, taking notes while on the road or on long walks, largely leading a life of solitude with only a few friends, a life of incessant travel. Kierkegaard mostly stayed put in Copenhagen, but, like Nietzsche, he was a brilliant stylist and a no less brilliant satirist who lampooned the academic philosophers for conceptual castle-making while real life transpires in rather more humble quarters, and he was even harsher with the theologians.

Although they never heard of it, Kierkegaard and Nietzsche are the founding figures of the confounding thing that was later to be called postmodernism. They are a sight to behold: philosophers making a philosophy out of attacking philosophy, philosophy as anti-philosophy, not simply critically delimiting its pretensions but really attacking it, ridiculing it, laughing at it. We are not sure if they are doing philosophy differently or if they are doing something altogether different than philosophy. We are not even sure if we should call them philosophers, if doing so is anything more than showing mercy to the librarians who must find a place to put their many books. The only thing of which we are sure is that, either way, they are incommensurables, different, and indeed it is the right to be different that concerns them, the right of the singular individual to beg to differ from the crowd that is forming under the name of modern European civilization. Neither ever married and their tormented relationships with women offer psychologists and psychoanalysts infinite material for study. Kierkegaard brooded endlessly over a broken engagement while Nietzsche fell for women who were interested in his ideas but did not have romance on their minds. Perhaps this is as it should be. Perhaps their suffering and solitude were the conditions of their work.

Among their many innovations, one that I especially treasure is that Kierkegaard and Nietzsche introduced laughter into their books, which represented an unprecedented break with a humourless philosophical tradition. (Kant is said to have written jokes into his lectures to lighten the heavy German tone, but they fell like rocks.) Truth cannot be heard, felt or appreciated without laughter, which breaks down the walls within which philosophers had immured their anaemic impostor. Emancipated from the normalizing protocols of university writing – they did not have to worry about getting tenure – their works were searing critiques and send-ups of European culture and thought. Europe, they thought, was moribund or fast becoming so, and they thought that truth required courage and hardness, the strength to endure: laughter in the face of the abyss.

You will quickly notice that Kierkegaard and Nietzsche were not democrats. Their politics are nothing short of appalling to the contemporary democratic sensibility. Nietzsche worried that universal literacy would level off reading to the lowest common denominator. Kierkegaard had contempt for the modern press and made frequent and brilliant sallies against the various manifestations of the levelling brought on by the media, and by the modern technological means of communication that were just beginning to emerge. They were troubled by the erosive, even degrading effect of the modern search for political freedom upon the general culture. They worried over modern egalitarian and democratic movements – the standardization, the trivialization, the levelling that keeps watch over the emergence of everything exceptional (don't even think of what they would have to say about the internet). To be sure, lovers of democratic freedom can use these criticisms to make for a better democracy, but they need to keep a constant watch on the rear-guard politics of these prophets.

Yet while each thought that the present age had become passionless, while they both wanted to restoke the fires of the passionate life, they had in mind opposite passions: Kierkegaard hailed the passionate faith of Abraham and the Christian martyrs, Nietzsche the pagan passions of the Greek tragedians, the 'tragic sense of life'. They each thought life a radically gratuitous event – why was I not consulted (about being born)? Kierkegaard complained. Nietzsche treated life as a piece of cosmic chance, of stupid cosmic luck; Kierkegaard as the grace of an inscrutable but providential God, of divine love. Nietzsche is one of the most brilliant, eloquent and unrelenting atheists the West has ever known. He is the philosopher who infamously declared: 'God is dead.' Kierkegaard, on the other hand, was the most brilliant brooding Christian writer of the last two hundred years. His reflections cut so deeply into the fabric of the human condition that not even the most cold-hearted atheists can think they have nothing to learn from him. By the same token, despite the virulence of Nietzsche's attack on religion, the insults he heaped upon it, his complete contempt for the religious psychology, religious thinkers return to him again and again for inspiration. Both mounted furious attacks upon Christianity, the one in the name of Christ, the other in the name of the anti-Christ. Tellingly, the attacks were pretty much the same: Christian Europe is sick. Kierkegaard wanted to restore Christianity to the health of its apostolic fervour, while Nietzsche sought to expose it as a disease to be wiped out. They advocated what Kierkegaard called the passion of 'existence' and Nietzsche called the passion of 'life' (we'll see why the choice of words makes a difference). But whatever their differences truth, they both agreed, is not a matter of thinking but of *existing*, of *living*. Not of books but of blood.

Kierkegaard

Truth among the Bourgeoisie

In *A Concluding Unscientific Postscript* (1844), the author, one Johannes Climacus (the most important of the many pseudonyms used by Kierkegaard), tells us that his vocation as an author came to him of a Sunday afternoon in Frederiksberg Gardens, while puffing on a cigar:

> ... wherever you look in literature or in life ... you see the many benefactors of the age who know how to benefit humankind by making life easier and easier, some by railroads, others by omnibuses and steamships, others by telegraph, others by easily understood surveys and brief publications about everything worth knowing, and finally the true benefactors of the age who by virtue of thought systematically make spiritual existence easier and easier and yet more and more meaningful – and what are you doing?... You must do something, but since with your limited capabilities it will be impossible to make anything easier than it has become you must, with the same humanitarian enthusiasm as the others have, take it upon yourself to make something difficult ... when all join together to make everything easier in every way, there remains only one possible danger, namely,

the danger that the easiness would become so great that it would become all too easy. So only one lack remains, even though not yet felt, the lack of difficulty.[28]

Kierkegaard was one of the first philosophers to live in a city that bore a real resemblance to a modern city, and he was the first one to say that the dizzying pace, the rushing hither and yon, the omnibuses, railroads, steamships, newspapers and telegraphs, pose a threat to truth. As these conveniences facilitate everything – travel, information, communication, thought itself – they threaten us with the real danger that things are becoming too easy. The difficulty is the lack of difficulty, which robs life of its substance and depth. The results for truth will be a disaster – a passionless truth, weak and weary and watery, as easy to come by as smoking a cigar in the park, and just as vaporous. The story of truth here reaches a turning point. The train has left the station on thinking about truth as an abstract philosophical idea. No philosopher before ever worried that truth was suffering from anaemia, and no one before had ever thought about truth in terms of railroads and omnibuses and telegraphs, in terms of city life.[29] Can we imagine Kant penning a passage like this?

To be sure, mid-nineteenth-century Copenhagen was of a modest size (population 125,000) compared to the London or Paris of the day, in no immediate need of an underground, and a longer way still from the cities of the twenty-first century. But Kierkegaard had his ear to the ground, and he had a prophetic sense of what lay down the road, of what was happening to European culture in the nineteenth century and hence, of what was going to happen to life in the age of advanced information and transportation systems. Nineteenth-century Copenhagen was a microcosm, an outdoor experimental laboratory, still walkable from one end to the other, a city he was able to scrupulously observe in frequent perambulations. The city had a prosperous harbour, a thriving commercial life, was in the midst of an intellectual and cultural golden age (the age of Hans Christian Andersen) and, as the capital of Denmark, was home to a thriving aristocracy. Copenhagen had a fashionable shopping district and could even boast of having the world's first theme park, Tivoli Gardens, which was just a short walk from the centre of the city. This Climacus denounced as a curiosity, a source of diversion, a transient entertainment that makes eternity look boring; an illusion that substitutes constantly changing externalities for inward growth which give a deeper joy to life.[30]

Kierkegaard was born in the heart of this city, the son of a man of considerable intelligence who was, if anything, even more brooding than his famous son. The father was a successful merchant and the family lived on one of the city's most fashionable squares, next to the courthouse and in the middle of the city's vibrant culture. His father left Kierkegaard a comfortable inheritance which gave him independence and allowed him to subsidize the publication of his books, which was a good thing given that many of these books sold poorly. He did not need to earn a living as a pastor or a professor and that allowed him the freedom to mercilessly attack the shortcomings of those who did. Kierkegaard, who in many ways was a stranger in the world and an admirer of the Christian martyrs, was also a modern urban man who had the resources to take advantage of everything the city had to offer – from its excellent opera to wonderful shops and coffee houses, and the opportunity for an occasional getaway to the country or to hop on a ship for a week in Berlin. Kierkegaard proved to be an extraordinarily acute observer of this world, keeping a brilliant record of what Anthony Trollope would call 'the way we live now'. He could hardly have seen what was coming, the extraordinary transformations brought about by jet travel and the new information technologies, but he saw things clearly enough that his complaints are still ringing in our ears today.

In this modern and thriving city, he observed, the real truth of Christianity was all but dead, suffocated by the prosperity, commerce, distractions, gaiety and quickening pace of life. How was that possible? The Lutheran Church was the established religion, pastors were supported by the state, and the local cathedral was quite beautiful. The Church had everything it needed, from well-paid pastors to the latest in candles and prayer books. Precisely, thought Kierkegaard. Once, to be a Christian meant to put your life on the line, to be fare for lions. Now everything was easy, including becoming a Christian. Christianity – he was thinking mostly of Danish and German Lutherans here – had completely forgotten the cross of Christ and the paradox of the Incarnation. It treated its Christian heritage as one more adornment of its burgeoning Christian culture, where everyone was Christian and no one would have the poor taste not to be. It had converted the wine of authentic apostolic Christianity into the water of easy bourgeois Christianity. Everyone went to church on Sunday mornings, he said, bowing their heads devoutly when the pastor said 'without God a man can do nothing'. After the services were over they passed their Sunday afternoons at Frederiksberg Gardens, with its families boating along the canals and lovers holding hands and strolling in the magnificent royal grounds (Kierkegaard, alone, watching it all go by!). On Monday morning, they set about proving just how much they could do, with no thought or mention of God until next Sunday morning. This was what he called 'Christendom', bourgeois Christianity, where everything was safe and easy, and in which the everyday life of the average Christian was as good as Godless. If he had thought of it himself, he could have used

Nietzsche's line that God is 'dead', if by 'God' you meant a way of life, a living faith, a transforming event that changed everything you thought and did (which is the bite that the word truth has), where being Christian was more than just bourgeois respectability.

The Truth That is True for Me

When still a very young man, Kierkegaard wrote in his journals, 'The thing is to find a truth which is truth *for me*, to find *the idea for which I am willing to live and die*.'[31] With these words he set in motion a revolution in philosophical discussions of truth, but one that was not without precedent in the classical idea that the search for truth was part and parcel of the search for wisdom, for living a wise life. The difference was that what he meant by truth did not turn on Plato's distinction between the metaphysics of the true world and the apparent one, but between a true Christian life and a phoney one and, more largely – and this is why the non-theologically minded also take to Kierkegaard – between what Heidegger would call an 'authentic' life and a conforming, 'inauthentic' one. Kierkegaard was the first philosopher to raise the question: how does truth survive the erosive effects of the 'public'? He made a philosophical category out of the public, a distinctly modern phenomenon made possible only by the emergence of the media and modern city life. The 'public' is constituted by 'idle chatter', by what 'others say', where the idea is to be 'in' on what is being said and to pass the word along, where it is enough to say what others say while never actually thinking for oneself.[32] This reduced Christian faith to a hoax, a fraud, a theatre show, where true Christianity was nowhere to be found – its truth corrupted by bourgeois culture, a consideration hitherto unknown to philosophy.

His vocation as an author, therefore, was to restore things to their genuine difficulty, which was not exactly the business-as-usual of philosophy in the past. Kierkegaard was addressing neither propositional truth nor ontological truth but what he called 'existential truth'. Truth for him was not a matter of true beliefs but of believing and existing truly. The problem of truth for Kierkegaard was a matter of dispelling an illusion, puncturing the pretence produced by what 'they' say, when 'they' are no one in particular. The 'they' is in truth nobody, a phantom, a void and a vacuum, exercising an invisible dictatorship over the individual, a spectre created by the press, telegraphs, omnibuses and the habits of modern urban life. The public suffers from the illusion that truth is gained in a poll, which adds up the opinions of the countless unthinking masses and thinks that counts for thinking.

His challenge, to convince people to *become* what they had been lulled into believing they already *are*, was doubly complicated: first he had to disabuse them of the 'misunderstanding' under which they labour, that they already are in the truth (Christians), which they are not – whence the pantomime and mockery – and then to persuade them to take up the task of becoming Christian, which of course they thought they had done quite some time ago: everyone in their family was a Christian and they had baptismal certificates to prove it and no one had recently converted to Hinduism. It would have been exactly half the trouble to have arrived on a remote island where no one had even heard of Christianity and then to present the 'good news' to the inhabitants and take his chances. At least then Kierkegaard would be spared the misunderstanding, spared the task of convincing the natives that they are not already what he is urging them to become. On this point he modelled himself after Socrates, who began by first convincing the Athenians that they did not know what they thought they knew.

The basis of the misunderstanding, Kierkegaard thought, is that bourgeois Christianity had completely eviscerated the difficulty of being Christian in daily life, even as the Hegelians had eviscerated the difficulty of faith by treating Christian revelation as a nice story to be deciphered in the philosophy department. Christians thought the truth of Christianity was as plain as the nose on your face, and that one would no more not be Christian than one would show up at the opera in the buff. They had quite forgotten the paradox. Imagine that someone, holding forth of a Sunday afternoon in Frederiksberg Gardens, claimed to be divine, a God-man, and claimed to do miracles to back it up. We would ask the police to remove this public disturbance and recommend the poor man be institutionalized to see if the doctors could get to the bottom of his madness. If we remove the dulling effects of the nineteen centuries that had passed, and make ourselves contemporaries with Christ and his little band of apostles, we might restore the difficulty, the trauma, the great paradox of Christ's appearance which requires us to fit together both a divine and a human nature, the creator of the universe and the babe born in a manger. In contrast to Hegel, who thought the figure of Christ was an image that could be clarified and smoothed out by philosophical concepts, Kierkegaard wants to sustain the tension and intensify the contradiction. To Kierkegaard, Christ was both a logical paradox (against the Hegelians) and a moral 'offence' (against the bourgeoisie) which repels our sensibility. By the latter he is referring to the utter scandal of God in the form of a common man: eating, sweating, getting tired and dirty, even the unmentionable aspects of tending to our digestive tract, and beyond all that, taking on the suffering and humiliation of a public execution as a common criminal.

Truth is Subjectivity

If Kierkegaard or his team of pseudonyms ever came up with a criterion of truth it would certainly have included blood, sweat and tears. Christendom is composed of tranquillized Christians, 'hollow men' as T. S. Eliot would later call them, people who have never doubted for a moment that they are true Christians. Kierkegaard's task as a writer is to disturb their tranquillity, to restore the difficulty of Christian faith, to persuade them that it is not enough to show up on Judgement Day with your baptismal certificate in hand, like an airline passenger trying to get through a security check. He is saying that whatever truth is, it does not come easily; it must come packing no small measure of fear and trembling. A real Christian is not one whose name is recorded in the parish registry but a Christian 'in spirit and in truth'. Truth means living it, *in truth*, verily, truly, which, said Kierkegaard, is not a matter of the 'what' but of the 'how'; not a matter of what you believe but of how you believe it. Truth, he said, is 'subjectivity', an 'existential' matter, a matter for the existing individual, who is what is really and truly 'concrete'. The word 'existential', of course, was destined for the history books. It took the German philosophical world by storm in the 1920s, then the French after the war, and finally washed up on American shores in the 1950s. But we cannot forget that the first people to seize upon the existential character of truth were religious: Augustine and Blaise Pascal (1623–62) were its vanguard and Kierkegaard was its poet, painting in memorable scenes the portrait of the existing individual alone before God (*coram deo*) – as opposed to sleepily reciting a creed at Sunday services or wearing one's religion on one's sleeve. Existential truth turned on the 'God relationship', on the white light of standing alone before God with all eternity hanging in the balance. In that light, the external circumstances of people – rich or poor, man or woman – are seen to be but a role played on the stage of time, an external costume worn by an actor, to be removed at death. Do not lace the garments of externality too tightly, he says. Remember, before God we are all equal, each one responsible for our eternal destiny, each one equally precious, which is why the modern idea of the 'individual' has Christian-Protestant roots.

Kierkegaard's view of truth turns on a famous distinction between objective truth and subjective truth.[33] In objective truth we dial down the existing subject to zero and put the accent on the object. Who the man is who claims '$2 + 2 = 4$' is of no importance to the objective truth of the statement. He may be bald or have a full head of hair, be tall or short, good or evil. He might even be lying, that is, he might stupidly think that this statement is false and that he is putting something over on us. Nonetheless, *what* he says is true, and his personal disposition is of no account in counting up to four. In existential truth the opposite is the case: we dial down the object to zero and put the accent upon the existing subject, so that no matter how true the statement is objectively, what matters is what Kierkegaard calls the 'subjective appropriation', *how* the existing subject is related to the object. For example, and this is not just an example, would you rather stand before God as a learned theologian who is full of pride or an unlearned man with a head full of superstition who worships in spirit and in truth? Kierkegaard was not denying objective truth, not denying that mathematics and astronomy had to do with objective truth; his point was rather that Christianity is not to be confused with an objective truth. For Kierkegaard, Christianity is an existential truth, meaning it must be realized in the way we exist in our personal lives, and the name of God is the name of a deed. The interesting thing is that, if Kierkegaard is right, the same thing would apply to the truth of any religious tradition, not just Christianity, which is the conclusion reached by postmodern theorists of religion.

Given Kierkegaard's idea of truth and his task as an author, his gift for satire, humour and dripping irony proved to be his method of choice. He valued laughter the way Descartes valued mathematics and the way Socrates valued stinging questions. While he insisted that Christ was a pure and perfect paradox, he also insisted that the philosophers and clergy were perfectly ridiculous. Kierkegaard divided his time quite evenly between lampooning the academy and the clergy. He got off some of his best lines dressing down the local professors, whom he thought were a long way removed from Socrates, and the local clergy, whom he thought were a long way removed from apostolic Christianity. For him, the philosophers occupy the especially ridiculous position of having forgotten that they exist, while the clergy earn a profitable living off the Crucifixion.

As Kierkegaard heard it, Hegel was saying that the passions of living individuals were simply the transient means of which the World Historical Spirit made cunning use as it coursed its way through world history. What matters is the result of individuals' lives, not their interior life, their personal motives, their qualities as individuals. Alexander the Great and Napoleon may have been personal monsters but even so, that is of no consequence to Hegel. All that matters are the objective consequences of their lives, which advanced the course of world history, mounting its ascent on the bodies of its victims. Many an innocent flower is tread upon by the march of the Spirit through history. For Kierkegaard this was proof that objective truth – here the objective truth of history – can corrupt. What matters is not the judgement of history but the judgement of God. For what does it matter if a man gains the whole world and suffers the loss of his soul? What matters is purity of heart, not world-historical results. What matters is not the place of the history of China in the march of the Absolute through time but the history of my soul, alone before God. The tension between the individual person and the Absolute intensifies the passion of existence, in which the individual makes decisions in time that reverberate for all eternity. We live before eternity, he famously said, while hearing the hall clock strike. The existing individual, what he called the 'single one', is neither a moment in the life of the Absolute (Hegel) nor an instance of a species (Plato and Aristotle). The individual is not a 'case' (literally a falling off from) of the universal, but ascends to the very summit of existential truth. What could matter less than the gossip and idle chatter of the press, which disapproves of the idiosyncrasies of the singular individual, to an authentic man who is true to himself? What could matter less than a show of wit at a dinner party (Kierkegaard himself), or a successful professorial career (he was denied one), or being elected a bishop (Kierkegaard's brother), or the history of India (Hegel), if the truth of inner man has been corrupted? What could matter less than objective truth if it comes at the cost of existential truth?

Kierkegaard's repetition of religion was directed at repeating the lost fervour of early Christianity, the time of the apostles and the martyrs, but such fervour risks ending up in a religious fever, a religious mad-

ness of its own. That is why I began by noting the
irony of invoking Kierkegaard to quell the madness
of pure reason – we are going to need a more bal-
anced critique of reason than this, one that does not
continue the war of faith and reason into which
Kierkegaard's knight of faith happily charges. Unless
it is carefully qualified, the task of finding 'the truth
that is true for me' seems one short step away from
the relativism that philosophers worry about. What is
singularly true for me is not necessarily true for you,
but how far can we go in that direction? We see the
first clear signs of trouble in his brilliant but disturbing analysis in *Fear and Trembling*[34] of the Bible story in
which Abraham is put to the test by God, who
demands that he sacrifice his beloved son as a sign of
his faith (Genesis 22). Here Kierkegaard defends the
idea that Abraham could on religious grounds 'suspend' the ethical prohibition of murder: Abraham
(and by extension anyone else) could take the life of
his son (and by extension anyone else), if that act were
indeed a sacrifice directly commanded by God. But to
counter the madness of pure reason with this kind of
religious madness is no solution. (In fact, there is
another, more ethical way to read the story of Abraham and Isaac, as a story of the end of human
sacrifice, but Kierkegaard would dismiss this as the
attempts of rationalizing academic biblical scholars
bent on escaping the bite of the Bible's message.)

Truth to tell, Kierkegaard is one of my heroes, one

of my passions, one of the reasons I undertook the study of philosophy. I will never be able to say how much I owe him. But I have to say that his idea of faith, in the end, even after every precaution is taken, would allow a parent to sacrifice an innocent child. It would break the parent's heart (that's why it's a sacrifice), but a parent faithful to God's command would do what God commands because of a faith that it is what God commands. Kierkegaard's God is a sovereign and inscrutable will (a lethal combination) whose commands are ours to obey, not to understand. To say that God is truth in Kierkegaard is to let all hell break loose.

We see this most clearly at the end of his life when he said that the point of Christianity was to put an end to sin, which came into the world through humanity, whose propagation depends on the sexual desire awakened by Original Sin, to which it is the duty of Christianity to put a stop. When an earnest young couple knocks on the rectory door seeking to arrange their marriage, the first duty of the pastor is to talk them out of it. But as usual the clergyman is more interested in earning an honorarium for the ceremony than in doing his Christian duty. This time the joke falls flat; Kierkegaard's scorn for marriage is sick and cynical. Celibacy is now made the rule, not the exception. Having taken to reading Schopenhauer, a philosopher who made his reputation as a pessimist and loathed the body, Kierkegaard was overtaken by the very 'sickness unto death' about which he otherwise wrote so brilliantly. His health in ruins, he collapsed and died shortly thereafter, already an old man at the age of forty-two, trusting the angels would escort this heap of bones into eternal life. This falls far afield of anything like wisdom and leaves us with a one-sided and in this way still abstract sense of truth, which collapses in upon itself. This was the very sickness with life brought on by Christianity that would worry Nietzsche, who launched a no less brilliant attack upon the decadence of European culture that is both the counterpart and counter-type of Kierkegaard. Of course, Nietzsche's final days are spent in even greater mental turmoil than those of the melancholy Dane.

Nietzsche

On the Road

Friedrich Nietzsche was the first major European philosopher to take extensive advantage of the modern railway system, which made it possible for him to travel around the south of Europe and to conduct his thinking on the road. He spent a rocky time as a professor of classics in Basel, a position to which he was appointed in 1868 at the astonishingly young age of twenty-four before he had even finished his formal studies, from which he finally resigned after ten years. His health was bad and he had no affection for academic life, nor it for him, as he had shocked the establishment in 1872 with his book *The Birth of Tragedy*, where his speculative musings over Dionysus and Apollo violated the conservative protocols of academic philological research.[35] After Basel, he took to the road for ten years of incessant travelling. Such travel would have been next to impossible without the new rail system, although his visits to small towns and remote places would have also required carriages and a fair amount of walking. Unlike Kant, who stayed in one place and constructed a magisterial system of philosophy, Nietzsche traded towns and hotels with astonishing rapidity and wrote in an almost completely aphoristic style. He deployed a dazzling dancing prose that leaped from topic to topic, dizzying readers trying to figure out how this all hung together, a problem that has kept philosophical scholars gainfully employed to this day. His life after Basel was fragmented and his work unsystematic, some would say ambiguous to a fault. All hail to the railroads. The modern system of travel available to Nietzsche made it possible for this wandering genius to wander in fact, to enact his love of change and becoming.

Each of Nietzsche's brilliant aphorisms lands like an arrow buried in our hide, piercing the veneer of what he mockingly called the 'true' world in Plato, the world of absolute and unchanging being. A multiplicity of cutting and concise aphorisms, a multiplicity of settings in Turin, Nice, Sils-Maria, Lake Como and numerous other European retreats, a multiplicity of forces – something like contemporary quanta in physics – summarized in a kind of philosophical abbreviation under the name 'will-to-power', misleadingly suggesting that there was just one such thing called the 'will' instead of a plethora of micro-forces in constant struggle with one another. His will-to-travel, his distrust of a system of pure reason, pits him almost perfectly against Kant, stuck back in old grey Königsberg. In the place of Truth, the hallmark of the philosopher from Plato to the present, he put a multiplicity of little truths, competing for their fifteen minutes in the sun of his notebooks, letters and eventual publications. At the height of his intellectual powers he was wandering about Italy and the south of France in search of a haven for his weak constitution and a place conducive to his writing habits amidst some of the most beautiful retreats in the south of Europe. He also loved to walk and write while en route. He is probably the first modern philosopher-passenger, and he used the railways the way modern academics hop from conference to conference on modern airlines. He made no bones about loving everything southern, sunny and warm, and that allowed him to gain some distance on his native Germany. He was a stranger in the world; an uprooted man who thought that at the foundation of things lies an abyss.

Truth is a Fiction We Have Forgotten is a Fiction

Given what the Platonic and Christian traditions were calling truth – he once called Christianity 'Platonism for the people' – Nietzsche said he would prefer fiction, falsity and opinion, thank you very much. He took his stand with life and he held that whatever truth means, it must serve the purposes of life or else it had no purpose, or worse, had a purely destructive purpose. While still a very young man he penned an essay entitled 'On the Truth and Lies in the Nonmoral Sense', in which he came up with a memorably perverse definition of truth, as far removed from Plato as he could possibly put it:

A movable host of metaphors, metonymies, and anthropomorphisms: in short, a sum of human relations which have been poetically and rhetorically intensified, transferred, and embellished, and which, after long usage, seem to a people to be fixed, canonical and binding. Truths are illusions which we have forgotten are illusions; they are metaphors that have become worn out and have been drained of sensuous force, coins which have lost their embossing and are now considered as metal and no longer coins.[36]

Truths are just fictions we have forgotten are fictions, a mobile army of metaphors on the move, trying to get something done. This was an extraordinary decision. Nietzsche didn't put truth first. He put life first and put truth to work in the service of life, which he took in the full range of this word, from its deepest biological sources up to sheer *joi de vivre*. He thought knowing the truth was like having teeth: it must serve some life-function, help promote the exuberance and flourishing of life. It was definitely not a goddess, and when he permitted the word divine at all, it meant life or laughter. He concluded that what is called truth in philosophy, where Greek philosophers like Plato have been allowed to call the shots, is more like death. It is useless for life, or worse than useless, and must be replaced with its opposite. In the history of truth, Nietzsche was a bombshell, a torch-thrower, a 'hammer', as he described himself. No one before or since has launched such an all-out attack on truth. Nobody ever dared to come out against truth or to claim truth did not come first. That would have seemed not merely ill-advised but mad, and at the end Nietzsche did end up mad, clinically. Were this not so tragic for him personally, we would be tempted to say it was a fitting ending for a kind of Romantic, or rather anti-Romantic hero, our candidate for the canary in the coal mine of modernity.

Nietzsche got the attention of the pious by famously

saying 'God is dead' (the pious retort, predictably, was 'Nietzsche is dead – God'). By this Nietzsche certainly did mean God, but not only God, if we may say such a thing. He meant the whole order of truth that had been put in place by the Greek philosophers and then joined in unholy matrimony with Christianity to produce the dreaded (for him) Platonic-Christian tradition with its system of opposites: being/becoming, truth/opinion, eternity/time, soul/body, super-sensible/sensible. He sought to throw these oppositions into reverse and take the side of the body and change, time and becoming, the lower or more disreputable member of the pair. This does not mean he always took the side of the underdog, since there were other opposites in the old order which he warmly embraced, such as master/slave, aristocrat/commoner, male/female. In fact he was famously elitist, patriarchal and anti-democratic, and he decried the French Revolution for having given the aristocracy a bad conscience. By going after the very roots of the western tradition, its most basic presuppositions, Nietzsche was a radical thinker with consequences both emancipatory (from Church and other-worldliness) and reactionary (anti-modern), but in any case he could not easily be boxed and labelled.

So what could it possibly mean for a philosopher to deny truth (a position that would never have got past the tenure committee)? First of all, in any straightforward sense, that would be logically contradictory because the claim 'there is no truth' would then be true, and therefore false. That is not only a contradiction in terms; it is the very definition of a contradiction in terms. Now since Nietzsche was a precocious genius and presumably knew what they teach in the first week of introductory logic, and what most people know anyway, he must have had something else on his mind, which I think goes something like this. *He did not let what we mean by truth judge life; he insisted that life judge what we mean by truth.* He denied what philosophy called truth in the name of another idea of truth, one that must adjust itself to life, not the other way around. For example, whenever 'I' make a conscious judgement, Nietzsche thought that was not my 'I', but an underlying vitality, or life-force, or 'will-to-power', speaking and acting through what he regarded as the grammatical fiction called 'I'. The question was not whether the judgement was true or false, but what end it served – life or death. What is considered true is not the result of a dispassionate judgement but what serves the life-force or will-to-power. Gilles Deleuze, a brilliant twentieth-century neo-Nietzschean, puts it this way: whenever you come upon a judgement or a desire, ask who, or better what, is doing the judging or desiring. A truth is but a perspective adopted by the vital forces that flow through my body in their struggle for ascendancy. The field of truth is simply the composite of contending vital forces, some stronger, some weaker. So compared to Hegel, Nietzsche is a materialist, who is speaking about basic, physical and biological forces, not about a spirit. The idea of an evolutionary drive was congenial to him but he criticized Darwin's version of it, where organisms adapt to their environment. Nietzsche insisted that they dominated their environment.

One of the most interesting things about Nietzsche for our little story about truth is that, as I have pointed out, he is the first philosopher to dare attack Socrates, the secular patron saint of philosophy who was martyred for his love of the truth, whom Kierkegaard considered a pagan antecedent of Christ. Nietzsche thought Socrates got what he deserved from the people of Athens because he went about making healthy and creative people ill, making them feel inept, stupid and guilty because they could not answer his questions about the definition of the things they did.[37] He who could not hammer a nail in straight made gifted craftsmen, people who could perform magic with their hands, feel bad because they could not define their art. Socrates did the same thing with statesmen and warriors, thereby robbing the *polis* of all its resources, of all the people that contributed to its well-being, and this because of their failure to cough up a theoretical definition of what they could do so well – as if that mattered in the least. Socrates would probably have humiliated Michelangelo and Mozart for the same reasons. Socrates failed to see the people he was humiliating had a know-how that did not answer to his philosophical idea of truth, and that the fault lay with him and his nihilistic conception of truth. The lasting damage Socrates did was to persuade Plato of all this, discouraging a magnificent writer who proceeded to burn the tragedies he had written as a young man and become a philosopher in the Socratic mould. Indeed, Plato became *the* philosopher, the one who set the accepted idea of truth in place, with its standards of unchanging being and timeless verity, with its ideal essences and pure forms, all expressed in the conceptually clear definitions Socrates sought. Then Platonism joined arms with the other-worldly forces of Christianity, with its flight from earthly life, and the rest is history – the history of nihilism (Platonic Christianity), as Nietzsche saw it.

Beyond Good and Evil

Since the first order of business for Nietzsche was to revalue the value of what the tradition called morality, he was happier if you called him an anti-moralist or 'extra-moralist' in search of what lies 'beyond good and evil' (beyond morality). That gives us an even more robust sense of Nietzsche's radicalism. He not only attacked Socrates. He not only sailed into truth. He also laid waste to morality. He thought these inherited philosophical categories, both truth and morals, represented a refusal of life, an attack on life, a twisted and inverted form of life, so that his inversion of Christian Platonism was an inversion of an inversion, and hence a righting. What the Christian Platonists call ethics is a morality of and for slaves, of and for dog-like fawning beings who are beneath the contempt of a real man, which he called his *Übermensch* (let's say 'overman' since 'superman' has been pre-empted by Clark Kent). When you read Nietzsche, you have to realize he means these things and he does not mince words. He divided the 'slave moralities', those that go down with the ship, those that go under (*unter*, as does the sun), those who are defeated by life's midnights, from the 'master moralities', the morality of those who 'go over' (*Über*), who ride out the tempests of life, those who think that life is justified (made worth it) by its high noons, so that one moment of unqualified joy, of exuberant life, justifies all the suffering. This is a bracing thought for the individual, a call to hold up under the worst, but as Nietzsche was of a deeply anti-modern and aristocratic temperament politically and culturally, he also applied it to culture at large. He thought that the high achievements of a culture, above all its art, justified whatever misery was being endured down below. The base structures of a society (the slaves who do the work) brace and support a social order and serve to free up its higher-order expressions.

Truthfulness

Nietzsche would have held in contempt a contemporary politician who panders to the mob and is willing to say anything in order to win their votes, up to and including baldly lying. He would have held in contempt a man who cannot be counted on to keep his word, who is not a man of honour, who is not true to his word, or a cowardly liar who is afraid to speak the truth. *What* truth? He has just finished denouncing truth. He means the truth of truth-telling, of being-true, of being trustworthy, of speaking and acting truly, of 'doing' the truth, a truth analogous to a craftsman's sense of when a line is 'true' (plumb), or to artists who are true to their vision. These examples represent what Nietzsche calls truth*fulness*, a concrete, living, vital truth, a sense of nobility, aristocratic magnanimity, of being-true, of being honest, which goes hand in hand with his critique of philosophical truth, which for him represents a lie, a falsification or denial of life. Nietzsche is profoundly incredulous of or suspicious about everything that the Christian-Platonic tradition calls truth, which he thinks is phoney, a cover-up, springing from a life-denying, nihilistic impulse, a downright fear of time and change, of looking mortal life in the eye, or of staring down into the bowels of the abyss.

So we have here a new model of truth: not the

truth of the Platonic-Christian tradition – the one where truth is in solidarity with the great chain of being – and not the truth that is subject to the rule of Reason in the Enlightenment. Truthfulness is the truth of suspicion, a cold and unvarnished truth, a suspicion of life-denying motives simmering beneath the surface of the rhetoric of truth, defending a kind of underground truth or truthfulness which suspects that what has been called truth up on the surface is a lie, what Jean-Paul Sartre would later call 'bad faith'. What Plato and the philosophers called Truth really means a refusal to be truthful, to face the truth, to admit the cold truth, which means that life is more abysmal, more groundless, more uncertain, riskier and more dangerous than those who put their faith in Reason or in the good 'old' God are willing to admit. If you want to see what is really going on, you have to look down, not up, go down the stairs into the dark corridors of the underground, get down in the mud, feel about in the bowels, and search the dark subterranean abyss for the hidden forces that hide beneath our skin, a project that would also be carried out soon after in Freud's explorations of the unconscious.

Nietzsche is a turning point, or doorway, to the postmodern, and in some sense even the post-philosophical, in which a rather different idea of truth is emerging. If we asked Nietzsche for a self-description, he would say he was a 'psychologist' of the religious and philosophical mind, a reader of its hidden motives, who sorts out the sick from the healthy, the base from the noble. The force of his thought rests on the persuasiveness of the portraits he paints, the capacity he has to make religion and Platonic philosophy look bad, and to expose the dark motives underpinning our prim and proper bourgeois lives up here on the surface of modern life. It does not rest on a knockout metaphysical argument (philosophy), divine revelation (religion) or modern physics (science). He does not use modern science to debunk religion as a fiction. He thinks science too is a fiction, albeit a useful and productive one as opposed to Christianity, which is a destructive fiction (except to the extent it kept the masses in their place). He recognized the monsters and demons by which we are disturbed and it was his task to expose them in their cold or brutal horror. He was the advocate of a kind of cold truth, an unflinching truthfulness, which was a condition for him of the unconditional affirmation of life. Truth for him is something we have to face, something with which we have to struggle, something we wish would go away and leave us in the tranquillized peace of everyday amusements and superficial distractions so that we might not notice that we are going to die; indeed we might not even notice that we, like our God, are already dead.

Eternal Recurrence

Nothing illustrates the well-known ambiguity of Nietzsche's aphoristic and highly metaphorical style better than his famous theory of 'eternal recurrence'. Eternal recurrence is the mythic idea that the course of time will be repeated over and over again, and has already been repeated an infinite number of times. So readers face a confusing situation: why is this critic of religion and metaphysics flirting with an old myth that goes back to an ancient Persian religion (Zoroastrianism) to get his point across? Considered by many to be Nietzsche's most important book, *Thus Spoke Zarathustra* is a powerful hymn to the body, the earth, time and becoming.[38] Zarathustra is portrayed as a kind of anti-Christ, who makes periodic trips down from his mountain to preach an anti-Christian 'good news' of the love of the earth rather than of dying and going to heaven. Zarathustra is tormented by a dark thought, something he knows but will not say, something that steals upon him betimes unawares but which he will not let escape his lips. Finally, at the beginning of Book III, this wandering preacher comes upon a horrid midnight scene of a young shepherd writhing on the ground struggling with a black snake that has crawled into his throat. Zarathustra shouts to the youth 'bite, bite', and the youth heeds his counsel and bites off the head of the serpent. Never, Zarathustra says, have I seen such exultation, such joy and laughter, such exuberance than on the face of that shepherd. Never have I seen life, the will to life and still more life, explode with such intensity, turning the midnight into high noon, and I longed for the joy of the shepherd.

As Nietzsche explains to us, the book is an allegory in which the black serpent stands for the thought of eternal recurrence.[39] Zarathustra is grappling with the idea that this life, this exact same life, this moment, this midnight, this shepherd and this serpent will recur again and again for all eternity, and indeed has already occurred an infinite number of times in the past. This is what Zarathustra means by the eternal return of the 'same', meaning the infinite recurrence not of a general pattern in history at large but of exactly the same life we are now leading. But why so much struggle with this idea? Because this thought suggests a terrible fate – that we are condemned to repeating the same cycle, that all is eternally the same, that all has already become and nothing is truly new. But this seems to contradict everything Nietzsche was seeking, namely, overcoming the Platonic-Christian tradition by way of a new breed of thinkers, the 'philosophers of the future', who will put slave morality behind them and become strong, healthy lovers of the earth. Thus the greatest test the philosopher faces is to love this fate (*amor fati*), to affirm the whole circle of becoming, the endless repetition of both the high points (Greek tragedy) and the low points (Christianity) of the cycle, all of which will return again and again. Zarathustra must embrace the idea that the same cycle of slave morals and healthy masters will be repeated endlessly, like the endless cycle of midnights and high noons. The final triumph symbolized by the shepherd is the acceptance of the eternal circle, an affirmation of life that accepts the fact that there is no escaping the circle of eternal return. Every escape from slave morality will be followed by its return. We have to take the low with the high.

There are many different ways to interpret this tale and the idea of eternal recurrence. The best explanation Nietzsche gave of it, at least the one that makes the most sense to me, is to treat the doctrine as a test of our own personal will-to-power, by posing a hypothetical question to ourselves: What if a spirit were to come along and whisper the thought of eternal recurrence in your ear? Would you regard this spirit as an angel or a devil? In other words, would you, in your heart of hearts, be willing to live your life – exactly the same life, in the same body, with all its joys and sufferings, bright days and dark nights, with all the truly mean, stupid and humiliating things you have done – repeated down to the last exact and most minute detail, repeated again and again, for ever and ever, as it has already been lived an infinite number of times before? Do you say *yes* to life – not an illusory blessed life in heaven where we don't get sick and old, but *this* life, with all its warts and bruises, all its ups and downs?

Do you say yes not to eternal bliss outside time but to the endless repetition of your life in time, to the whole wheel of becoming, all its sufferings and all its joys bundled together in one package? Take it (life) or leave it. Are life's sufferings justified for you by its joys (Greek tragedy), or is life damned by its sorrows and death (Platonic-Christians)? Do the high noons of life justify its darkest midnights? The story of eternal recurrence provides a criterion or a principle of selectivity that sorts out the strong from the weak, the best from the worst, the noble from the base, the lovers of the earth from the lovers of death and an illusory after-life. Read thus, eternal recurrence is an 'existential' truth, an existential test, a hypothetical thought experiment that measures what's in our bowels, not a speculative metaphysical theory about, or religious revelation of, the essence of reality. It belongs to the domain of *existential* truthfulness.

Henceforth truthfulness demands we take life on its own terms, without requiring any divine insurance policies that all is well or will eventually be well in the end, affirming life in all its glory and misery, the two together, which divides the yea-sayers from the nay-sayers. The same essay I cited above, 'On the Truth and Lies in the Nonmoral Sense', starts off with a remarkable late modernist image:

> Once upon a time, in some out of the way corner of the universe which is dispersed into numberless

twinkling solar systems, there was a star upon which clever beasts invented knowing. That was the most arrogant and mendacious minute of 'world history,' but nevertheless, it was only a minute. After nature had drawn a few breaths, the star cooled and congealed, and the clever beasts had to die.[40]

Nietzsche actually exercises quite a bit of a prophetic power here, catching sight of something found in the Big Bang theory of contemporary physics, that the expanding universe is headed for thermal equilibrium, accelerating ever more rapidly into entropic dissipation. Our local sun is flaring up and burning out so that at some point half a trillion years or so from now the earth will be toast. Nietzsche makes a comparably grim forecast of cosmic weather, in the face of which he advises the affirmation of life, be it ever so brief and short-lived, ever so tragic and difficult.

In the upbeat version of eternal recurrence he gives at the end of *Thus Spoke Zarathustra*, a young man is dancing with a lovely young woman ('life'). They whirl around and around the ballroom and when the music ends, the young man says, 'Was that life? Well, then, once more!' – not from eternal frustration or disappointment with life but from joy, that life is justified by its highs, however low its lows may be. That I think is the right conclusion to draw and it is quite the opposite of what the youthful Nietzsche had said in the earlier text, that after our cosmic flare has burned out and humanity will have disappeared, 'nothing will have happened!' On the contrary, what has happened is life, and life is not refuted by death but made all the more precious, and we are like lovers making love in the night because in the morning they must part. Life is justified as an 'aesthetic' phenomenon, he concludes. By this he means not merely by art, although that is part of what he means (like a lot of post-theists, he thought the old religion was to be replaced by art). More importantly, he was saying that life is justified by our feeling (*aesthesis*) and passion for life, and that passion is self-validating. He was saying life is justified by its high points, and that life itself divides the high from the low, the noble from the base, the strong from the weak, and serves not as a scientific or objective criterion of truth, which would require proofs and evidence and arguments, but as an existential test of truthfulness – to life.

In sum, the theme of rationality that sprung up in modernity, which set Reason up in judgement over God and truth and detached itself from the classical search for wisdom, eventually ended up looking foolish. That in turn occasioned a kind of anti-modern blowback. The first reaction took the elegant form of Hegel's metaphysics of the spirit, in which the formality of Enlightenment rationality was absorbed as an abstract moment into the concrete life of truth in history. The next was the searing and sarcastic attacks of Kierkegaard and Nietzsche, who countered Enlightenment rationality with the passions of existential truth and of a pagan affirmation of natural life, of the earth and time. But Hegel's thought remained complicit with the modernist notion that there is nothing to which reason does not have access. Kierkegaard's thought ended in a kind of sickness unto death and allowed our life in time to be shattered to pieces by the shock of eternity. Nietzsche's affirmation of life was shockingly elitist and aristocratic. By the end of the nineteenth century, we were left with a choice between the madness to which Pure Reason had led and a salutary madness which had reacted against it. But either way truth remained within the grip of the dichotomies set in place by the Enlightenment, of faith versus reason, rational versus irrational, subjective versus objective, certitude versus doubt.

By questioning the assumptions common to both sides, twentieth-century philosophers opened the door to a new way of thinking about truth. In taking a postmodern turn, philosophers would show that these dichotomies were in fact straitjackets that make it impossible to understand what we are doing, that they in fact gave rise to a kind of blackmail – if you are not for what the Enlightenment calls Reason, you are judged irrational. That is like saying if you are not for the policies of the party currently in power, you are unpatriotic. They demonstrated that the borders between these opposing categories break down, that faith is a way to see even as seeing requires a certain faith. In the emerging view of truth that would take shape under their hand, which is modelled after neither God nor Reason but the event, to be in the truth is to be mindful of the contingency of what we take to be true at any given moment, and to cultivate an acute sensitivity to the unforeseen turns truth may take in the future. In short, to be in the truth means to stay in play with the event, and that requires willingness to take a risk. There thus emerged a postmodern sense of truth that was a counterpart to the ancient idea of wisdom; a sense of truth cut to fit a more chaosmic world in which things move at dazzling speeds – and all of this was foreshadowed by the complaints lodged by Johannes Climacus about the omnibuses, telegraphs and steamships that so disturbed his inner life.

6. Truth in the Postmodern Situation

In the twentieth century the wheels came off the bus of the Enlightenment. In a century that was witness to a series of genocides perpetrated by both the political left and the right – totalitarian politics keeps unnerving company with theories of Absolute Truth – and the lethal brinksmanship of the nuclear arms race, no one was in the mood to hear that history is the unfolding of Truth, of God's life in space and time, or that things are guided by the rule of Pure Reason. That can't be right. Anyone who has ever ventured past the front door knows that life is obviously a lot riskier than that, that there's a lot more in play, and hence that what we call truth is a more elusive thing. The shock delivered by these events, which rocked the politics of the twentieth century, proved no less of a shock in the world of arts and letters. So it should not come as a surprise that it sent philosophers on both sides of the Atlantic back to the drawing board. Hereafter philosophers were a lot less likely to think of reality in terms of smoothly running trains on tracks, or the unfolding of a deeply lodged

Truth, be it God's or Reason's rule. They became more attuned to the irregular than to the rule, to the discontinuous rather than the linear, the hybrid instead of the pure, the singular rather than the universal, the marginal over the mainstream, the shadings and the mixtures instead of the clear and distinct, and a lot more willing to concede that things can, and do, go wrong all the time. This did not mean jettisoning the idea of truth, by any means. It meant complicating it, redescribing it in less wistful and idealizing terms, with a sharp appreciation for the twists and turns that truth can take, and presenting it in ways that were often ironic, parodic and iconoclastic. That is pretty much the tone taken in postmodern times, which goes hand in hand with living in a world of blazingly fast electronic communications, global markets and global travel, constant movement and relocation, multi-tasking and hyperlinking.

The time had come to thank the old Enlightenment for its services, present it with a gold watch as a token of our gratitude, and bring in new blood. The tidy axioms of the Enlightenment had come unravelled, even as the axiom that God is truth had become confined to sermons. The time had come to look for an alternative to God and Pure Reason. That alternative, as I proposed earlier, and which I am calling the postmodern view of truth, turns on the idea of the event. Events are disconcerting, but they do not spell pure chaos. The event allows for reinvention while the forces lined up against it aim at preventing the event. The event is what we are referring to every time we protest against being done in by a rule – 'but this time it is different'. The difference, the idiosyncrasy, the unprogrammability, is the event. What is singular is not irrational; it requires discernment, not simply the application of a rule. A computer can apply a rule, but it takes judgement to decide what is demanded by the singularity of a situation. If the event is the core of the postmodern view of truth, as I have said, it needs to be fleshed out in more concrete terms to show how it is at work in everything from ethics to physics. From this larger story I will single out three highlights, in which I will try to distil the postmodern way. The first move, called 'hermeneutics', was made by French and German philosophers under the lead of Martin Heidegger; the second was the idea of 'language games' introduced by Ludwig Wittgenstein, the legendary Cambridge philosopher (born in Austria); and the third is the idea of 'paradigm shifts' developed by Thomas Kuhn, a Harvard historian and philosopher of science.

The Hermeneutic Turn

The one word that I think best sums up the postmodern turn is 'hermeneutics', which means the theory of interpretation.[41] I treat hermeneutics as the key to the postmodern mutation in the idea of truth and I think that 'language games' and 'paradigm shifts' presuppose a hermeneutic theory of truth. Interpretation is the pin that pricks the balloon of absolutism once and for all, and denies Pure Reason its over-inflated privileges without landing us in the ditch of relativism. I say this despite the fact that it looks like the opposite. Surely, to lower the case and the volume of Truth all the way down to interpretation is to court disaster. To say everything is 'a matter of interpretation' is to throw truth under the bus of relativism, to reduce it to somebody's opinion, to open wide the door of subjectivism, passion and the irrational. The Big Bang is just somebody's opinion, while the Baptists out in Kansas have their own opinion called Creationism, which is just as good. It's a free country. Everybody is entitled to their own interpretation.

So what is an 'interpretation' and why is hermeneutics not just the sceptical brush-off we hear in saying 'it's all just a matter of opinion'? Take a typical crime drama on television. When an innocent person is 'framed' the villain has created a context in which the innocent person is made to appear guilty. The defence consists in producing an alternate frame under which everything the apparently guilty person did is redescribed – the incriminating evidence was planted, the accused was at the scene of the crime but had just arrived there on other business, etc. But the crucial point is this: either way, there is a frame – the 'frame up' and the reframing, the right frame and the wrong.

Now call the frame the context and we can jack this up into a philosophical principle: nothing is ever context-free *and* nothing is immune to being recontextualized. The battle waged between the prosecution and the defence is a hermeneutic battle between competing contextualizations. Great lawyers are great recontextualizers, great hermeneuts! Hermeneutics explains why *Law and Order* had such a long run – all hail hermeneutics! There can be no higher praise!

We call the move made in hermeneutics postmodern because it sets out in exactly the opposite direction taken by Descartes in his search for absolute certitude and the universal rule of the mathematical method. Descartes tried to doubt everything, to clear his head of every possible presupposition which might prejudice his view of the things themselves. In hermeneutics, that is considered a little mad: the truth is gained not by approaching things without presuppositions – can you even imagine such a thing? – but by getting rid of inappropriate presuppositions (frame) and finding the appropriate ones, the very ones that give us access to the things in question. Nothing ever happens outside a context and nothing can be understood without a set of presuppositions within which things are properly or improperly framed. The ideal of presupposing nothing adopted by modern philosophers like Descartes is making an ideal of an empty head. *'Absolute' knowledge absolves itself of the very conditions under which knowledge is possible in the first place.* Presupposing nothing results in know-ing nothing. The contest is not between absolute and relative, which is the bill of goods modernity tries to sell us, but between more plausible and less plausible 'readings' or contextualizations. That is why an inno-cent person can always be made to look guilty, or the opposite, why juries sometimes get it wrong, and why covering theories sometimes cover up. We should not be trying to presuppose as little as possible but to pre-suppose *enough*; understanding requires a robust and sensitive set of presuppositions tailored to the demands of the subject under investigation. Having a robust set of presuppositions that casts things in the right light is what hermeneutics calls an 'interpret-ation', which is a far cry from 'merely a matter of opinion' – or of simply doing the maths. Interpret-ation is a matter of insight and of sensitivity to the singularity of the situation with which we are con-fronted, rather than of submitting the situation to a set of inflexible rules laid down in advance by a Method or a pure fiction called pure Reason.

We require a flexible notion of truth and reason but one that still has teeth – we obviously need to be able to say things are right and wrong in ethics and in physics – without driving ourselves mad with method, or just plain miserable and mad, as Kierkegaard and Nietzsche. I am saying that the dichotomy 'it's either absolute or it's relative' (rational or irrational) is a ruse, a trap. So we have to get rid of it. I am not trying to strike a middle position 'between' the absolute and the relative. I am not trying to split the difference; I am trying to move 'beyond' ('post') both positions, or rather to slip back behind their lines and challenge the presupposition that is common to both. That, I propose, is exactly the work that 'interpretation' does for us. Absolutism supposes that truth must be presuppositionless; relativism agrees that that indeed is what truth is, and adds 'but that's impossible' so think what you like. Hermeneutics says truth is not a matter of presuppositionlessness but of having the right presuppositions and avoiding the wrong ones.

If we wait for absolutes to fall from the sky, nothing will ever happen. If a general waits to be absolutely certain about the time to charge before he gives the order, his forces will be overrun. But if he thinks that any time is as good as another, the results will be no better. If lovers wait for absolute certitude before they pledge their troth, fewer and fewer troths will be pledged; but if they swear undying love after the first date because they have half an idea this might just work out, the divorce rate will spike. We don't get Cartesian certitude in romance, sports, warfare, the stock market or even in shopping for fruit. The idea is not to find a midway point between absolutism and relativism but to scuttle entirely that oppositional schema, which has done so much damage. Modernity's obsession with certainty is hard-headed and it's blackmail. Access to truth is less like the soul contemplating pure forms in Plato's upper world and more like people who through practice have cultivated a trained eye – for art, for true friends, for scientific theories or for picking fruit at the market – and make better choices, for the most part, but not always. Postmodernists think that truth is a matter of good interpretations and bad, good reasons and bad, productive insights and dead ends. Nothing is guaranteed or, as Žižek says, there is no Big Other. We can't expect God, Nature, Pure Reason or the corner grocer to offer guarantees. Facing up to such straits is, in an interesting way, the only way not to abdicate our responsibility. As Derrida was wont to point out when he was accused of being irresponsible because of his avant-garde ways, the opposite is the case. Looking for a rule to follow is the height of irresponsibility; we are trying to avoid making a decision so we can then blame it on the rule. (We were just following orders – a lamentably lame excuse.)

The word hermeneutics comes from Hermes, the Greek god of messengers and messages. With the advent of Christianity, Hermes lost his job to his biblical counterpart, the angels, even as the angels, I think, are losing their jobs today to smartphones (although polls in the USA say angels are still inordinately popular among the American faithful).[42] Nowadays, the word hermeneutics is a kind of umbrella term for a wide variety of theories of interpretation. To say something is true on this account is to say that at present this is the best interpretation we have, our best take on the truth, our best perspective. There is no truth without interpretation but having an interpretation does not make it true. As a friend of mine said, we do not want to end up in some kind of ever-churning relativist gyre (my friends talk like that). In a democracy, where people are entitled to their own opinion, we cannot report to the police those people who think (or blog or tweet) that truth is just a matter of opinion, nor can we invoke a recent encyclical from the Pope. But we can make their opinion look bad on purely interpretive (hermeneutic) grounds, where we have replaced 'pure Reason' with what philosophers today call 'good reasons'. We can show up bad interpretations with good interpretations. By saying 'good' and 'bad' we are not moralizing or impugning motives; we just mean plausible versus implausible, fetching versus far-fetched. We insist that some interpretations are better than others, more fruitful and felicitous. That is not relativism, but it does acknowledge that truth, like life, is a risky business, with the crucial added proviso that what is even more dangerous is to try to remove all the risk.

For example, we have our hands full nowadays with a spate of religious fundamentalism claiming equal rights with science – everybody is entitled to their own opinion! – concerning things such as the theory of evolution. Far from being condoned by hermeneutics, this claim is a hermeneutic disaster, awash in hermeneutic confusion on at least two counts. The first is biblical hermeneutics (which is actually where the word was first used). On strictly biblical grounds, Creationism is a bad interpretation of the opening chapters of Genesis, as any informed religious believer can tell you. It is historically anachronistic and ignores the character of biblical narratives, which are religious stories, parables, or even poems, not modern scientific treatises. It makes the wrong presuppositions about the text and it makes a bad decision to reduce the text to its literal meaning. It is important to determine literal meaning, but 'literal*ism*', the idea that this is its *only* and exclusive or normative meaning, is a gross error in reading. Literal reading is a first word, not the last. The Scriptures, like any text, have many levels of meaning, only one of which is literal. In the Middle Ages, which respected the resonance of the Scriptures, they said the Scriptures contained multiple levels of meaning – literal, moral, symbolic, mystical, etc. Augustine said let there be many different interpretations of Scripture so long as all of them are true. As a matter of fact, many people regard the sometimes exotic interpretations of classical texts found in Derrida as a trademark of Judaism. His playful style is anticipated by ancient and medieval Jewish Midrash, where the rabbis stood on their heads trying to outdo one another with exotic interpretations of the Bible. What we call 'the' Bible is a misleading translation of *biblia*, multiple books and scrolls, in the plural, from many different times and authors – 'the' creation story, for example, is a composite of two different ones, separated by several centuries – that lend themselves to multiple layers of interpretation. In short, when someone says 'this is the word of God', that is someone offering us an interpretation of what they mean by 'God' and by 'word' and a reading of what they think 'God' is 'saying'. In hermeneutics everything could, in principle, end up in scare quotes. Hermeneutics is scary stuff. The second hermeneutic disaster in Creationism's claim to equal time is that it is terrible science where interpretations are called theories. Theories are big deals and not easy to come by. If you do come up with one you'll get your name on it and become one of the scientific immortals. So the Big Bang is not 'merely' a theory which opens the doors to any alternative theory one would like, say Young Earth Creationism (the world is only 10,000 years old). Rather, the Big Bang rises to the heady level of a genuine theory while Creationism does not. Why not? Because Creationism contains an untestable hypothesis (interpretation) concerning an immaterial being (God) outside space and time which cannot be measured in the language of mathematics or tested by empirical experimental methods – otherwise known as the God of the gaps. The whole thing fails the test of scientific interpretation; it does not *rise* to the level of a scientific theory. It is not a false or alternative scientific theory; it is not a scientific theory at all. In fact Creationism is as bad an interpretation of the Bible as it is of science and at this point in the hermeneutic game we say that there are no good reasons to hold it. It has neither biblical nor scientific grounds to stand on. We can make such arguments as clearly and as often as possible, but we cannot, would not, call the police, or bomb the buildings where creationists construct their arguments, or burn their books or exile them to a distant isle.

It is worth mentioning that the ill-conceived approach taken by the creationists, to treat the Bible as a competing scientific theory, confirms my earlier point about the degraded character of the category of 'religion' concocted in modernity. Those religious believers who oppose such things as evolution are, if I may say so, aping the very modernity against which they are so violently reacting. They have contracted an advanced case of Cartesian anxiety and the search for absolute certitude. They have swallowed the modernist idea that truth is strictly a matter of propositions and the result has been that they shrink faith down to combative proofs for the truth of religious propositions. This does a disservice to religious experience and it only succeeds in producing a poor send-up of science or reason. The Protestant concept of the 'inerrancy' of the Bible (literalism) and the Roman Catholic conception of the infallibility of the Pope (certitude) are fabrications of modernity; they are what is called in religion 'idolatrous', and in psychoanalysis, a 'fetish'.

They depend entirely upon modernist assumptions about truth. They were constructed within the framework of modernity in order to counter modern naturalism and atheism with a kind of religious counter-certainty and counter-modernity – but they are the sworn enemies of religious truth.

An interpretation is a way of construing things, of having a 'take' on them, which casts things in a certain light, fits them within a certain framework or horizon, for better (when it is felicitous) or for worse (when it is ham-fisted or contrived). Interpretation requires what we variously call judgement, discernment, or insight. We have to be judicious, skilled in adjudicating competing perspectives and in negotiating differences. In all this, we will lack for hard and fast rules to rule some things in and others out. In the postmodern world, which is awash with multiple means of communication, it happens, too often, that the people making the interpretation do not know what they are talking about – Kierkegaard and Nietzsche were particularly prescient on this point – although they know enough to get online. The internet is a nest of interpretations unworthy of the name, even as it is also immensely informative and emancipatory, an ambiguity typical of postmodernity that we just have to learn to live with. *Wikipedia* is a good example of an ongoing postmodern truth process which invites public input while also making an effort to monitor the reliability of what is posted there. Behind the scenes of most *Wiki-*

pedia entries you'll find a host of lively debates about the accuracy of their content, which are the work of unpaid editors and contributors. But *caveat lector*, reader beware, you still have to be a discerning reader of electronic publications which lack the usual protocols of journalism and academic refereeing. There are plenty of bargains on the web – authentic Picassos for less than the price of a new pair of shoes, but how do you know they're authentic? It says so on the internet.

The important thing here is that we want to be able to judge the difference ourselves, not just individually but also collectively, and we trust the dynamics of dialogue and debate to get us somewhere, without believing naïvely in the idea of undistorted communication. We do not want the police or the Church telling us the difference. Interpretations require insight into the material; they have to be earned and learned. The risky thing about interpretations – which comes up right away when we use expressions like 'a matter of interpretation' – is that they don't derive from a rule. If an interpretation succeeds it may result in a rule, but we don't have a rule for coming up with rules, and the rules we do come up with only last until we run into the next exception, which requires a fresh interpretation. Rules don't go all the way down. But interpretation does – that's hermeneutics, in a nutshell. Interpretive skill in the face of situations that are not ultimately rule-governed – that is the heart of any sensible idea of reason, truth and wisdom in the postmodern condition.

The cash value of the idea of interpretation is that it supplies a third thing that lies beyond the great modernist divide, the fixed oppositions, the either/or categories of absolute vs. relative, rational vs. irrational, subjective vs. objective, and the knock-down winner-takes-all battle to acquire certitude and abolish doubt, all wars waged to the death by the Enlightenment. The advantage of interpretation is that while absolutes are nowhere to be found, interpretation is everywhere. Scientists make their way by interpretation, by proposing testable hypotheses that are a tribute to their insight and expertise. By the same token, an ethical decision arises from an interpretation of the idiosyncratic demands of the situation, in which the universality of the laws of ethics heralded by Kant lose their teeth and we are required to exercise some insight into the singularity of the situation – as opposed to the foolish advice that Kant gives us to always tell the truth, no matter what – even if you are protecting an innocent person from a murderer who knocks on your door and asks if you are hiding him!

Artworks are, and demand, interpretations. Detectives investigating a case have to interpret clues and whether people are lying or telling the truth, and when we get to the trial the judge and the jury have to interpret how the law applies to the present situation and whether the defendant is lying through his teeth. All the while the lawyers are interpreting how the jury is reacting to their arguments. Our lives depend upon doctors interpreting symptoms. Teachers interpret the subject matter to the class as well as the response the class is making to the lesson while the class is interpreting what the teacher says. A tennis player tries to read her opponent's strategy as well as the direction and velocity of the ball in just the way a golfer tries to interpret the play of the wind or the slope of the green. Politicians 'spin' the facts in their own favour so we have to take the spin into account in interpreting what they are saying.

A common conversation is a delicate work of interpretation, because we have to construe not only the meaning of the words that the other person uses but also a host of non-verbal clues such as facial expressions, intonation and body language, which is why a video is superior to a transcript. On the telephone we have to immerse ourselves in a disembodied voice. The blind develop an exquisite sensitivity to voices and sounds. We can get computers to 'read' formal languages but it is much more difficult to 'teach' computers to discern the non-formalizable features of a conversation (although there has been a lot of unnerving progress with this lately). Every time we go shopping it is an adventure in interpretation, judging cost, quality, utility, deciding whether we should seize the moment or whether this is just impulse buying. Interpretation happens anywhere. We seem to do it naturally, which is good, because interpretation is truth in action.

So, too, we bid a happy adieu to the rigorous divide that modernity tries to enforce between faith and reason. An interpretation is not a matter of following rules but there is nothing irrational about it; it requires faith but it is not a matter of religious fanaticism or blind faith. In any interpretation faith and reason work hand in hand. Instead of Absolute Truth, we ask for insightful interpretations; instead of Pure Reason, we want good reasons, ones that do a lot of work for us and may hold up for a while. We put a lot of trust in good interpretations, and trust is confidence and confidence means faith (*fides*). Remember Derrida's repetition of Augustine: there is a faith that runs deeper than 'beliefs', like theism and atheism, and is the common root of both reason and religion. So an interpretation is neither arbitrary nor absolute. There is a good deal of faith packed into what we call reason and plenty of good reasons baked into the faith we have in our interpretations. A good interpretation is an insightful way of construing things. Bad interpretations, on the other hand, don't hold up, and sooner or later collapse in a heap, unless they are enforced by the powers that be (the definition of propaganda), by people with a vested interest in holding on to them. But we have to be careful not to throw the baby out with the bathwater. Just because people abuse power and enforce their interpretation of events (which is usually all about keeping them in power) doesn't mean that interpretation itself is to blame.

One way I have found of getting the opposition's attention in discussing hermeneutics is to deny that there are pure facts. There's the smoking gun, the friends of Absolute Truth conclude! Facts are facts and the hermeneuts are against facts! Truth to tell, if it is a 'fact' we like to think it is true, but that does not make it a 'pure' (uninterpreted) fact or an absolute. (Hint: 'pure' would mean no context!) On the contrary, the only way to establish a fact is by way of interpretations. Even the word 'fact' (from the Latin *facere*, meaning 'to make') gives this away. In the most literal sense, facts are made (*factum*), and here we hit upon another sense of 'making the truth'. That in turn makes the true blue friends of Truth red in face. The conversation grows more heated! The word 'fiction', to which we like to oppose facts, has an analogous etymology, from *fingere*, *fictum*, to 'form', and in hermeneutics we are perfectly happy to say that facts are formed, which means not pure of and uncontaminated by fiction. We do not distinguish between formed and un-formed, but between well-formed and ill-formed, or between informed and uninformed, or between risky unconformity and being too conforming. The friends of the Absolute rend their garments and look up to heaven for relief. But consider the matter more carefully. Consider the cold facts about cold facts. In order to come up with facts, we have to make a contribution to the cause and do our bit. They will not show up at our door when we need them if we have not paid our annual dues. Facts help those who help themselves. We are saying that all understanding is interpreting; to understand is to understand something *as* such and such. Without the 'as' nothing happens, nothing comes into view. The 'as' supplies the frame, the context, the right presupposition. Trying to understand the world without the 'as' is like using a remote whose battery is dead. You cannot change the channels; you cannot even power up.

Ask yourself, for example, how many facts are there right now in your kitchen? We greet the question with a smile; it makes no sense. Why not? Because we have not done our part. We have not managed yet to ask a serious question, even though, like the politicians, our lips are moving. That is because we have not specified the frame of reference. Facts are a function of the frame of reference that picks them out, which means that there are no pure uninterpreted facts of the matter. But if we reframe the question to ask, how many knives are found in your kitchen?, we can come up with an answer, hopefully the right answer, the one determined by how many knives there really are. Of course, there are no guarantees; nothing says we won't miss the knife hidden behind the dishwasher, or that a dispute won't break out about whether the potato peeler counts as a knife. Facts are always checkable, revisable, recontextualizable, redescribable, reinterpretable. The best information we have at the present means the best interpretation. Accordingly, to deny that there are pure facts is not to deny our access to reality, but it is to deny a lot of nonsense that works itself up into a fury over the spectre of relativism while entertaining the illusion that truth drops into our laps from a goddess in the sky.[43]

The search for 'pure facts' will yield no reality at all, whereas the well-formed interpretive search for sufficiently specified or framed facts will cut through the confusion to the facts. Making contact with pure uninterpreted facts – and here we use an example from Kant – is like the illusion suffered by the dove which thinks it could fly all the more freely but for the wind that gives it such resistance. An interpretation is not a wall between us and reality, but a window in the wall. The better formed or framed or made the interpretation, the further we see out the window into reality, in exactly the way that the better polished our glasses, the better we can see; the better the automobile, the further we will be able to drive. The more we make the truth, the more truth gets made. An interpretation is not subjective if that means arbitrary or locking us inside our heads. Far from it. An interpretation gives us an angle, meaning an angle of entry into reality, like a spacecraft which can re-enter the earth's atmosphere without burning up only if it strikes exactly the right angle. A student in a stupor about a pending assignment has read the material (we will be generous in our interpretation) but has no angle, no entry, no interpretation. To lack an interpretation is to be left without a clue. Without an angle, the student needs an angel.

In order to reach an understanding of something that is free of interpretation, we would have to drop the 'as' and decline to adopt a perspective or an angle. That is called adopting the 'view from nowhere', or God's point of view, the view from everywhere. We would have to be omniscient, omnipresent and eternal. That is exactly why postmodern philosophers accuse modern philosophers of posing as gods, trying to assume a God's-eye view of History or Nature, instead of conceding that we are all 'poor existing individuals', as Kierkegaard put it, meaning we all pull our pants on one leg at a time. That is also what was behind Kierkegaard's barb that Hegel is passing himself off as the 'absolute professor'. Back again to Lessing's preference for the left hand of God. God, in the traditional view, is pure being, whereas we are still stuck in becoming. We are finite, 'factical' beings, as Heidegger put it, meaning thrown into the world in a given time and place not of our own choosing and we start from there, like it or not. But that is both good news and bad: it both limits our perspective (we are not God) *and* gives us our point of view (we do reach an understanding). We all find ourselves situated in a particular space at a particular time, speaking a particular language with a particular set of assumptions and idiomatic tropes that are the product of a given moment in history and culture, with a language, a gender, a religion (or not), a home and family (if we are lucky), over none of which we had any say. That means we will always have a blind spot, the way we cannot get outside our own bodies and view them from without, *but we will also always have an angle*. Our situation does not merely blind us, it unbinds us; it opens things up for us, gives us our perspective.

Because interpretations are not eternal beings that have fallen from the sky into our laps, they are capable of change, and explaining how such change takes place is among the most important features of interpretation theory. Most often the change takes the form of changes *within* the framework, refining and correcting the prevailing frame of reference, fine-tuning it as new events – new situations, unexpected results – pour in. But sometimes the changes take the more radical form of a change *of* the framework itself, when the framework or horizon of understanding undergoes a shift. Sometimes an event is encountered which the prevailing framework can accommodate, but sometimes it cannot and then things undergo an abrupt, discontinuous and holistic shift. This brings us to language games and paradigm shifts.

Language Games

While hermeneutics is largely a continental European development, things went no better for the old Enlightenment idea of pure Reason in Britain and

America, where logic, science and empirical investigation have always enjoyed pride of place. It was a cruel twist for the Enlightenment to be gutted right here in Anglo-America. *Et tu, Britannia?* The crack was spreading. What was splitting apart was the notion of Pure Reason, which implies that science, for example, obeys a pure logic, that its progress comes by steady incremental growth, each new discovery arriving as a linear addition to the preceding state of science, as pure facts assemble themselves before the eyes of disincarnate value-free scientific researchers following pure laws of evidence. But science does not drop from the sky. It is not the issue of a supraterrestrial species of bloodless, disembodied cloud-borne observers of pure and neutral facts, like the scientists at the 'Grand Academy of Lagado' in *Gulliver's Travels.*

The first shock occurred in England when Ludwig Wittgenstein (1889–1951) proposed his notion of 'language games'.[44] By games he did not mean amusements, but any rule-governed activity, and by languages he did not mean English, German or French, but the discourse proper to some sphere of activity. For example 'ethics', 'physics' and 'politics' are different language games, somewhat in the way we might speak of the 'life insurance game' or the 'art game' or the 'education game'. Each game has rules proper to itself and you can't judge one game with the rules of another, in just the way that you cannot call 'checkmate' in football. When the teacher tells the student 'you failed', the student really did, even if the student disagrees – according to the rules of the education game, unless they're actors in a movie, which is a different game. If this seems innocuous to you, think again. Wittgenstein was legitimizing the plurality of what he called the 'forms of life' and cutting off reductionist arguments – as when someone says that ethical judgements are 'nothing more than' neurons firing. Whenever someone says y is 'nothing more than' x, we hermeneuts head for the door. They are being reductionistic about x, shamelessly engaging in x-ism. Everything is x or a version of x – where x might be sex, science, religion, morals, economics, the unconscious or, nowadays, a computer program. Reductionism is cheating, mixing up the rules of one game with the rules of another. Physics and ethics, neurophysiology and art – they're all different games, sharing a certain family resemblance among themselves. How about religion, the frog in our ecosystem? Another language game, with rules of its own. Each one is a 'form of life' in which life is working itself out and something is getting itself said and done.

The postmodern twist is that there is no game of all games, no meta-game to which all the games report back, to which we can appeal to settle the disputes that break out between games. Each game has its own integrity. That means there is no Pure Reason but a multiplicity of reasons proper to each game, and we cannot judge one game 'irrational' by the rules of another game. So if the Enlightenment conceived of Pure Reason as a high court that adjudicates all disputes, Wittgenstein was saying there is no such institution, only a multiplicity of district courts regulating their own jurisdictions. Descartes said that mathematics is the universal model which every enquiry must imitate, be it physics, theology, ethics or politics. Wittgenstein begged to differ. Things are more complicated than that. Truth is like a winning move in a game, like checkmate in chess, but there are different rules for different games. As there is a plurality of games, so there is a family of truths, in the lower case and the plural, with standards proper to each sphere. There is no meta-language, no one trans-historical overarching game or rule or story, no high court of Reason, but rather a multiplicity of good reasons in multiple forms of life.

The upside of Wittgenstein's view is that it frees us from the illusion induced by the Enlightenment that science alone is rational and everything else is just emotions, and it describes instead the different ways we have of making sense (of having good reasons, behaving intelligently) in different contexts ('games') as different as physics and ethics. The downside of the idea is twofold. First, if you push too hard on the separateness of the games, then each game becomes an island and we are back to a new version of bucket-thinking and the modernist archipelago. The right way to take it is to keep the rules flexible and reinventable and to stress the 'family resemblance' among the games. Physics and ethics do not divide into rational or emotional (aka irrational); they resemble each other as different ways of behaving sensibly within differing frameworks. Secondly, if you put too much stress on the 'rules' of the game, it is a recipe for conservativism and conventionalism. For example, if the prevailing conventions or rules that govern saying 'I do' exclude same-sex couples, then what is required is a refusal to play by the rules and to push back against them, or, in the language of the event, an intervention upon the conventions, a kind of inter-inventionalism, rather the way fresh metaphors bend the rules of standard linguistic usage. That is why Derrida sometimes spoke of per*ver*formatives, performances that pervert or reinvent and thereby let the event happen, rather in the way we speak of 'gender-benders'. Sometimes the event takes the form of making a new move in an old game; but sometimes the event takes the form of inventing a new game altogether, like a work of art so avant-garde, so strikingly different that it leaves everyone asking, 'but is this art?' That confusion is salutary for Lyotard, a sign that something new is happening, something that might even lead to revolution. That is the event, and the perfect entrée for Kuhn's proposal of paradigm shifts.

Paradigm Shifts

First, Reason suffered a body blow from Heidegger's hermeneutics in 1927, then a shot to the head from Wittgenstein's *Philosophical Investigations* (1951); finally there came the knockout punch from Thomas Kuhn's landmark book *The Structure of Scientific Revolutions* (1962).[45] Kuhn was a historian of science at Harvard and he brought us the now-common expression 'paradigm shift'. The old Enlightenment went down for the count. After Kuhn, it would no longer be possible to ignore the element of historical context in science, meaning that science, like everything else, was the work of fellow travellers, of earthlings like the rest of us, with passion for and a faith in their interpretation. Kuhn argued that we will be misled about the nature of scientific truth if we concentrate on a pure logic without regard to the life of historical scientists.

The word 'revolutions' in the title of his book was used by Kuhn to signal a parallel with political revolutions. That sent a shockwave through the ranks of academic philosophers. Political revolutions, after all, are not very scientific. I say the philosophers were shocked because by and large scientists pay little attention to what philosophers say about science and simply go about their business undisturbed. They rarely mention philosophy and do not discuss truth –

at least not until they retire or are given an honorary degree and have to say something about science as such. (My own bet is that if you could get them out of their labs long enough to talk about what they are doing, they would be highly amused to hear that anyone ever thought they were *not* fellow mortals.) The disturbing thing about the political analogy is that political revolutions are led by men and women driven by passions, or even by a spontaneous and unruly mob stirred up by an unfounded rumour, which means they could therefore be waged for the worse, not for the better cause, and they depend upon luck and circumstance for success. Just so, Kuhn acknowledged; science and politics are not as purely opposed as we have been taught to think by the Enlightenment, not if you check out the historical facts of how science goes about its work, or rather – and the emendation is crucial – how scien*tists* go about their work. The suggestion was so scandalous that Kuhn was accused of turning science over to 'mob psychology'.[46] Kuhn lit the fuse of the defenders of the old Enlightenment. He might as well have told them they had to go back to church and be born again. His heresy was to defy the central dogma of modernity: that Reason is not to be confused with faith or feelings, and if it is, the result will be 'irrational'. Science, Kuhn is saying, is of a more supple stuff. Rational and irrational are straitjackets.

To see what Kuhn is getting at, suppose we woke

up one morning to find that someone had discovered a new and hitherto unknown novel by Dickens in their attic. That would be news aplenty; it would make literary headlines. Hordes of Dickens experts would converge on the manuscript, testifying to its authenticity and telling us what it adds to our already considerable knowledge of Dickens. But how would a discovery like that compare with what happened when James Joyce published *Ulysses*? That was certainly literary news, but it created turmoil, threw the critics into confusion, and left a lot of people asking, is this really a novel? Is it even art? We couldn't ask the experts to resolve the problem because, truth to tell, they had never seen anything like it before and couldn't agree among themselves. What Kuhn came up with was meant to address a problem like that, which he found by studying the history of science and we now have reason to think can be found anywhere.

Kuhn's hypothesis is that the state of scientific research at any given moment is organized around the prevailing paradigm, by which he meant an established set of scientific practices which the masters of the discipline have perfected, and in which apprentices in the trade are to be initiated, which regulated what he called the 'normal' state of scientific practice at the time. So a paradigm is like an interpretive framework or a language game; it supplies a stable matrix for particular practices. Normal scientific work lies in filling in the missing pieces, making incremental refinements to the existing paradigm (framework), taking Newtonian physics to the next decimal point, as they said in the nineteenth century. Kuhn is certainly not saying that normal science is a vast desert of uninspired, routinized robots repeating what they were taught in graduate school. Scientific experiments deal with scientific events, with singular results, not with routinized and indifferent data. Accordingly, the best practitioners of normal science are marked by the passion and inventiveness with which they move around *within* the paradigm, making it dance, so to speak, so the paradigm stays alive, on the move, and makes progress. But overall this progress is linear and incremental because the experimentation remains within the borders marked off by the paradigm, which it progressively corrects and confirms. The shock of truth is thus delivered in measured doses, in adjustments and corrections, dealing with puzzles but not falling into vertigo.

This is to be distinguished from times of scientific 'crisis', which occasion holistic or revolutionary shifts in the entire framework of assumptions that govern the existing paradigm. We see this in the profound conceptual shifts – or shocks – delivered by Copernicus, Newton, Darwin and Einstein (a list of what Hegel might have described as the world spirits of science!). For example, Darwin introduced a paradigm shift in biology, whereas the latest discovery of a fossil that alters the dating of *Homo sapiens sapiens* corrects, refines and fills in the already existing and still standing model of anthropogenesis, the scientific reconstruction of the origin of the human race. Paradigm shifts are bigger, harder to come by and rarer than that. The furthest thing from Kuhn's mind, and this is what his critics missed, was to suggest that paradigm shifts would occur easily, that paradigms could shift arbitrarily, or that they can happen every day. Indeed, everything about the momentum of science as he describes it resists such shifts, and rightly so; Kuhn objected strongly whenever anyone, stampeded by the spectre of relativism, suggested otherwise. That means, Kuhn said, we have to distinguish 'revolutionary' science, which is extraordinary and thankfully rare, from normal science, which is not. This distinction effectively replaces the old one between absolutism and relativism. In normal science, the day-to-day work of science, the best scientists are better at doing what everyone else can more or less do; in revolutionary science, the best scientists are doing something that no one else is doing. In normal science, the paradigm is stable and is assumed to be correct, so that when experimental results come in that contradict the paradigm, we cling to the paradigm and greet the anomalous results with scepticism. In terms of the political metaphor, that scepticism is the genuinely conservative streak in Kuhn's theory of revolutions. It almost always results in showing that a mistake was made in the experiment or, if not, that the results reveal a higher, hitherto unknown law within the system which refines and ultimately reinforces the prevailing paradigm.

There are recent examples that illustrate how resistant standing paradigms are to shifting. In 2011, there was a shocking report that the speed of light, the one absolute in the universe, is not so absolute, that in fact neutrinos, particles with almost no mass at all, can travel faster than the speed of light. That claim was greeted with an appropriate amount of scepticism, and the challenge has since been put down by experimenters working at the CERN particle accelerator near Geneva. That is as it should be, Kuhn would say, because normal science is the norm, the stable state of the art, the most well-established and best-supported account we have, and science cannot tolerate having a great deal of careful work thrown into daily crisis. In 2012, Fabiola Gianotti, a CERN physicist who was part of the team that had confirmed the existence of the Higgs boson particle that year, said that the discovery of this particle actually achieved two results: 'One is to give [an explanation for how particles acquire] mass. The other is to prevent the standard model from going bananas.' This is a good way to formulate Kuhn's notion of normal science. Scientists do not like bananas. They do not want and cannot tolerate having the current paradigm going bananas.[47]

But bananas do happen. Occasionally, an anomalous result – an event – is so intractable that the current paradigm is thrown into question, which is what would have happened if the neutrino results were repeatedly confirmed. Then physics would go bananas, or in Kuhn's terms, this would occasion a scientific 'crisis', which is the occasion of a 'revolution', which means a 'paradigm shift', an expression so suggestive and felicitous that it has worked its way into our everyday vocabulary and has been widely adopted in other disciplines. The crucial point to grasp for the idea of truth is that paradigm shifts can happen anywhere. Luther precipitated a comparable crisis in theology, Picasso in painting, Cantor in mathematics, and on and on. Human practices do not divide into rational (science) and irrational (everything else), but are each marked by a distinction between normal and revolutionary that cuts across them all.

Now back to Dickens and Joyce. The discovery of a new Dickens novel – an event – would fill in our knowledge of Dickens, but the genre of the nineteenth-century British novel or the subgenre of Dickens Studies (the hermeneutic framework, the Dickens game) would be left standing, refined and expanded but not thrown into crisis. That is what Kuhn would regard as incremental or normal development and Lyotard would call, again thinking of Wittgenstein's language games, a new move in an old game. Joyce, on the other hand, invented a new game altogether; he effected a paradigm shift, delivering a shock to the literary world of such proportions that the novel and literature itself would never be the same thereafter.

So how are crises resolved? If you're looking for a rule, prepare to be disappointed. What rules in times of crisis are not rules but noses, someone with a nose for the future of science, for example. Right now superstring theory is ripe with explanatory power, but is empirically unconfirmed and unable to generate predictions. But a lot of people believe (in) it. Then is this mob rule, just as the critics object? Of course not. It is much more like calling in an expert when everyone else is confused because the usual rules do not work. One reason paradigm shifts are so hard to come by is that the proposed new paradigm does not emerge from nowhere, but from a discontent with the existing framework by its experienced practitioners representing a new way of seeing *as*, of looking at things (interpretation, hermeneutics). It requires an inordinate and intimate acquaintance with the existing paradigm, the state-of-the-art science of the day, even to experience such discontent, and a still more extraordinary inventiveness to imagine an alternative. So while it is not rule-driven there is nothing arbitrary about a paradigm shift. Crises are not resolved with rules, because it is the rules that are in crisis. They are resolved with discernment, judgement and interpretive acumen.

Indeed, scientific revolutions represent the exercise of a creative and elemental scientific intelligence which is feeling about for the nerve of intelligibility in the phenomena. This represents a much greater show of scientific intelligence, let us say of 'prescience in science', than is to be found in the practice of normal science, which does not challenge the prevailing paradigm. Aristotle called it *nous*, insight, not *logos*, reason, which he said is also required if we are to have wisdom (*sophia*). It is scientific intelligence glowing white hot, but it is not the rule-governed rationality of the Enlightenment. The perplexity brought about by the anomaly (the event) is critical but it is not irrational. This perplexity is a happy example of the hermeneutic situation where a breakthrough gradually gathers a consensus, the experimental evidence is gradually multiplied, until finally the hoariest advocates of the old paradigm agree, retire or die. The dissidents who bet – there is a certain amount of poker playing in science, too – on the new paradigm were in the vanguard, and history makes those who thought they were playing it safe by betting against it, who denounced it as irrational or irreverent, look bad. *Or* the new paradigm dies away because no evidence comes in to confirm it, no one else can use it, and history proves the advocates of the existing paradigm to be in the right. Truth is a risky business.

I don't agree one bit with the critics who think this is relativism (nor did Kuhn), but I do think that we postmodernists, who suspect fixed oppositions, are obliged to weaken the opposition between paradigm shifts and incremental shifts. These are, after all, matters of scale, of how far we zoom in or zoom out. Writing revolutionized oral communication; typewriters revolutionized handwriting; and word processing revolutionized typewriters. Since then a series of incremental shifts led to the word processing programs of today which make our old 1984 Macintosh look like a different animal altogether. In 2007 Apple introduced the iPhone that revolutionized what was previously called a telephone. Since then Apple and its competitors have rolled out a series of incremental shifts that eventually will add up to another big shift compared to the first smartphones. Then at some point another large leap will be made of a more transforming nature, followed by more rollouts. And so it goes in science or technology – and in art and ethics. What counts as a paradigm shift or an incremental shift depends upon the frame of reference we assume, the scale on which we are thinking, on whether we are tracking short- or long-term arcs of change.

The larger point that interests me lies in thinking of truth in terms of events. Events are shocks to the system or the framework, sometimes small and medium shocks that take place inside the prevailing framework, and sometimes big shocks to the frameworks themselves. That explains my fondness for heretics. In my work on religion I turn to the mystics and the dissenters and those who generally pose a pain to the orthodox framework or establishment. My

heroes are heretics and whenever I encounter orthodox dogmatic theology I suspect the worst. So Kuhn
is a hero for me because he was guilty of high heresy
against the Enlightenment. The furious reaction he
elicited would have been worthy of the Inquisition.
After Kuhn, everything was different, not because
everyone became a Kuhnian – then Kuhnianism
would become the orthodox theology – but because
he had dared enter the very citadel of 'reason', the
physical sciences, and violate the purity of the goddess, Rationality. After Kuhn one ignored the concrete
historical situation of the working scientist only at
one's peril.[48]

Kuhn himself represented a kind of event or paradigm shift, a shock in his own right. The passionate
reaction against him by the Enlightenment rationalists,
stampeded by their fear of relativism, served perfectly
to confirm what he is a saying – that science is deeply
embedded in a passionate search. Passion is why anybody would care about science to begin with. That is
also why defenders of cold Enlightenment rationality
get hot under the collar whenever their conception of
cold truth is challenged. After Kuhn, we began to
think about science and scientists in ways that
were more historically concrete (Hegel), existential
(Kierkegaard), passionate (Nietzsche) and interpretive
(Heidegger), all because of the event. Kuhn's heresy
was to argue that when science experiences surprising
about-turns, something that seems 'impossible' within

the existing framework of possibilities, it requires a certain faith and passion to see it through. To be sure, the wing nuts, like the poor, will always be with us. There will always be foolishness. There will always be people like the Young Earthers who propose things that are simply outlandish. But we should not let our frustration with such people stampede us into a Cartesian anxiety and a search for absolutes with which to bash them. I can only repeat that the most we can do with them in a hermeneutic-democratic order is make their arguments look bad. We can't call the police or have them silenced.

The most interesting work in the philosophy of science today, in my view, is being done by Ian Hacking (1936–) in the Anglophone world, and across the Channel by Bruno Latour (1947–), a French historian and sociologist of science, both of whom try to balance the historical component (somewhat controversially condensed into the word 'construction') with realism.[49] Science certainly sinks its mathematical teeth into reality, but Hacking and Latour argue that this means we need both reality and teeth. In short, nothing happens without inventive constructions, but constructions are not 'mere' constructions, in the same way that theories are not 'mere' theories. Obviously human beings are not responsible for gravity but for 'gravity', that is, for the concept and the theory of gravity. But without the theory – and this is why we need people like Kuhn, Hacking and Latour – gravity is lost on us. We have access to reality only under the conditions written into the theory by its authors, which is why the theory has a history and can be altered, not arbitrarily as the Friends of the Absolute fear, but in the fallible and risky way that science (and everything else) has always followed. We retain the right to alter scientific laws the way we insist upon the right to throw out elected politicians. Good science, like democracy, requires a theory of events.

As I've mentioned, the idea of paradigm shifts is immensely fertile. The crucial thing to see is that it applies across the spectrum of disciplines and beyond academic enquiry. It lays to rest the blackmail enforced by the old dichotomy between absolute truth and relativism or the false choice between the rational and irrational. When Marcel Duchamp placed a urinal on a pedestal in 1917 and declared it a work of art, we can variously say he effected a paradigm shift (Kuhn) in contemporary art, or changed the rules of the art game (Wittgenstein), or recast our interpretive frame (hermeneutics), all of which for me are alternate ways of speaking about events. He provoked a debate about what art is, whether 'anything goes' in art. We do not know at the time whether the innovation has legs, whether it will amount to nothing or transform the practice of art forever after, and the experts do not know either; nor do they get to call the shots. In art, as in anything else, we cannot see what is coming, which does not mean that anything goes. Picasso visits a museum exhibiting African masks. Afterwards nothing is the same in twentieth-century art. The first works of Cubism were greeted with derision by the establishment. The *New York Times* ran a competition mockingly offering ten dollars to anyone who could identify the violin in Picasso's earliest works. The rest is history and the *New York Times* eventually swallowed its pride and got on board. The collector Alfred Barnes amassed a fortune in Impressionist and Post-impressionist paintings because the establishment of that time considered them rubbish. This does not reflect a simple disagreement but a clash of paradigms. The disagreements were not simply differing judgements within a shared framework of reference but a difference about the very framework itself. The two sides reflect differences about whether this is art at all! If it is a genuine paradigm shift in art, it will catch on, produce a movement, and generate a critical mass of practitioners along with a community of taste. In just the same way, if it is a genuine paradigm shift in science, empirical confirmation will start to appear, other scientists will pick it up and use it to solve other problems, and it will become the new state of the art in science. If that does not happen, the old paradigm will prevail and the innovation will collapse.

The same result can be seen in ethical life. Ethical life has a conservative tendency. We tend to resist change in ethical norms because they are close to our heart. Such a tendency is even stronger in premodern societies, when transportation and communication were difficult and the local traditions were all most people knew. Then the major problems were casuistic, meaning, deciding 'cases', figuring out how we apply the norms we all agree on to particular cases. But occasionally the ethos is visited by a shock, not simply a different and difficult case, but an exception that throws into question the entire framework. At a certain point, the most ancient standards of patriarchy were called into question with results that were as repugnant to the old guard as questioning geocentrism was to the Church (which suffered the disadvantage of defending the wrong side on both counts). In general, the Church has a lousy record of dealing with events. Eventually we realized that 'all men are created equal' actually meant 'all people are created equal', which explains the shock felt when abolitionists advanced the claim that there is no 'natural slave', an ancient idea as self-evident to Aristotle as it was to St Paul. Similarly, the American Bible Belt is traumatized by challenges to the idea, as ancient as the Appalachian Mountains themselves, that heterosexuality is the truth of sexuality. Such traumatic transformation is facilitated by the accelerated pace of life today, when travel between countries and continents is commonplace and when our knowledge of history and biology has been vastly enlarged and new information is immediately sent speeding along electronic highways into even very remote places.

Now we have a clearer sense of the difference between the truth of propositions and a larger, more encompassing sense of truth. It is one thing to determine assertions that are correct and incorrect judged against a received standard of rectitude – an existing framework, a prevailing paradigm, the rules of a language game. This gives birth to more determinate but lesser or more restricted truths. It is quite another matter when the standard itself trembles, when the very framework is in question, when someone invents a new game, or as I like to say, when an event happens. Then a larger or more sweeping truth is at stake and the decision on this level eludes the rules of correct and incorrect, rational and irrational, and depends upon exercising judgement. On the one hand, there is the truth of 'correctness', of judging whether something is 'right' or 'straight' (*orthe*) judged against the measuring rod agreed upon by the community of practitioners. There is still room for events, for novelty and innovation inside the existing horizon or genre, language game or paradigm – like the excitement that follows the discovery of a new way to use the genome map to treat diabetes or heart disease. That novelty is what Derrida calls the invention of the 'same', an innovation within an existing frame of reference or horizon of expectation; this, he says, is the invention of the 'possible'. Against this, on the other hand, we distinguish the truth of a more radically shattering and transforming sort, when the entire horizon shifts or is shocked, when a new framework emerges, when the world is reinvented. This Derrida calls the 'invention of the wholly other', when the event is something radically unforeseen and unsuspected within the existing framework, within which limits we do not see it coming, do not think it possible. The first has to do with the possibility of the possible, the second with what Derrida calls the possibility of the impossible, the coming of the event in its most unfettered sense.

I cannot fail to point out that Derrida's language has a slightly religious tone here, since it evokes an old idea from the Bible that with God, nothing is impossible. If so, we might even see our way clear to repeating the old idea that God is truth, so long as the name (of) 'God' is taken to be the name of the possibility of the event, the possibility of the impossible. That has the advantage of situating the name of God on the side of the revolutionary instead of the reactionary, of temporal unforeseeability not of eternity, of becoming not being, and of the shock of the event rather than of the status quo. On Lessing's terms that would mean that God has two left hands, and in Hegel's terms that God is down here in the mix with the rest of us.[50]

Is it Still Possible to Love the Truth?

Is loving the truth still possible today? Have we become too cynical, too postmodern to fall for such a line? Is the search for truth and wisdom a sentimental quest best left to dead Greek philosophers? Or can we 'repeat' this idea in postmodern terms? I propose an idea of truth as a force that keeps the future open and is closely tied to faith and hope in the face of what we cannot see coming. I am calling for a ceasefire in the series of wars ignited by modernity – between the religious and the secular, faith and reason, theism and atheism – but no less between the humanities and science. What I mean by postmodernism is that these buckets leak, that these oppositions cannot hold up under scrutiny. Something more obscure and tantalizing stirs beneath the radar, an event which, perhaps for lack of a better word, I say has a certain religious quality. Let's say that I advocate a 'new covenant' (I do not claim to have coined that phrase), a covenant with the impossible, where religion means a passion for the impossible.

I locate the dynamics of truth in open-ended exposure, not a safe and closed system. We cannot really search unless we admit we're really lost. Life in the postmodern world is on the go, marked by an acute sense of change and uncertainty about where things are going. If the postmodernism I advocate can be called religious, it is a religion that will give little comfort to the faithful in the confessional religions. My postmodern religion demands people of faith, people of hope, who believe that the future is always better, in one way or another, whether or not they have any confessional beliefs. Otherwise the passion of contemporary life will be contracted into obstinate ideology; faith will be contracted into blinding, binding beliefs – unless, of course, one believes nothing at all. For by being endlessly on the go we live with the constant threat of allowing passion to be dissipated and distracted, consumed by a world of consumerism, degraded into self-seeking.

The love of truth belongs to the postmodern condition no less than to Greeks now long dead. But by love of truth I mean the excitement posed by the future, the openness of what we know to all that remains unknown, living on the border between knowing and un-knowing, truth and un-truth, the possible and the impossible. Human beings are border people, living in the between, in the transition from the present to what is coming. To be in the truth requires that we confess our exposure to what is not yet true. When we profess to see we must likewise confess that what we see lies exposed to the unforeseeable. What is present is exposed to what is coming. The event of truth re-discloses and reinvents our lives. It re-opens the world and transforms it and so transforms us, and our restless postmodern hearts.

Otherwise the present closes in around us and closes off the future.

The workings of truth spread into every corner and interstice of our existence, in science or art or politics or personal experience, in propositions and in the world that precedes and follows propositions, of which propositions are the distillate. When I speak of the love of truth, the *eros* or desire for truth, I am saying this is something we *are*, not something we decide to do. I am saying that the moment someone says this *is* the truth – this *is* democracy or science, sexuality or ethics – the *one true* interpretation, then the flow of truth is cut off, the borders are closed, the event is prevented, the life of interpretation is crushed, the future is shut down and replaced by anxiety about the future. The police of truth have arrived.

7. The Future of Truth

If we have learned anything at all from this trip, it is to let truth be, to let it lead so that we can follow. We never know what truth will do next, nor can anyone dictate to truth how it is supposed to behave. If so, then the obvious question is what lies ahead? Where are we going? What will we make of truth in the future – or better, since truth has a mind of its own, what will truth make of us? Just how far can truth be stretched – or will it stretch us?

In the terms set down in this little book of truth, and since there is nothing final or definitive about the postmodern, we are now required to ask ourselves, 'what comes after postmodernity?' Here I think we have to face up to many uncanny things, to drones and robots and cyborgs, to things so strange as to make postmodern hybrids like St Augustine and Derrida look tame. It is as if we have just woken up in the Mos Eisley Cantina in *Star Wars*. This future, for which we must prepare to be unprepared, is called 'post-human', meaning the technological supplementation and transformation of the very horizons of 'human' life and mortality.

Post-humanism, or What Comes After Postmodernity?

I counsel the reader to avoid concluding that we have reached the conclusion. Just the opposite. If the word truth exposes us to an unforeseeable future, no book is ever closed. It will always be necessary to say something about the future, to keep the book open on the future, to expose the book to the future. If I have dared to entitle this book *Truth*, that is not to be understood as if there is such a thing, one unified and finished thing that travels under that name, to which the reader is here being presented. Instead it announces a promise that lures us on and excites a journey; it calls for something to come. Accordingly, instead of meaning something conclusive and capitalized and reassuring, the word truth now inspires caution and modesty and even a bit of trepidation, a carefulness that avoids rushing to a conclusion, an openness to the unforeseen, a willingness to take a risk. So my final thought, which is far from a conclusion, is that today, as we speak, this situation of accelerating change has been compounded, intensified and magnified. Today, the outer horizon of travel has shifted from the intercontinental to the interplanetary. The measure of velocity is the speed of light. Today, good old *terra firma* has become Spaceship

Earth, destined to be turned to toast as the sun – which was for the ancients both the symbol and the substance of the immutable – flares up and burns out. The horizons of what we mean by earth and sun, space and time, by matter and even human life itself have begun to undergo a transformation whose measure we have not yet taken.

My parting question, then, is this. What will we – all of us, north and south, east and west, male and female, rich and poor – become in the face of a transforming future we can barely imagine? In the ongoing and incessant becoming-true of truth, what will become of us? Might the force of truth that is coming, that is already being felt, spell the end of the human and the beginning of something strange and unnerving? Are we at present poised on a precipice in which the human will be displaced by an uncanny and spectral successor form, for which what we have called philosophy and its love of truth is unprepared? To put my question as briefly as possible, what will humanity mean in a *post*-human age?

Post-human? What kind of beast slouching towards Bethlehem is that? Truth to tell, I am just bringing out something that you will all have noticed without any help from me – that the contemporary world is at this very moment in the midst of a paradigm shift of massive proportions. Our best guess is that what we call 'now' will hereafter be called the 'Information Age', or at least its onset. Information now flows with the speed of thought across the skies like the angels of old in the Bible, just as supersonic aircraft streak across the sky like angels in a Renaissance painting. Everything is being swiftly transformed and we are on the go with a velocity the like of which we have never seen before. Life even fifty years ago looks quaint, leaving teenagers to marvel at the hardiness of their grandparents who grew up using rough-hewn prehistoric tools like black-and-white TVs. People tote around smartphones with computational capacities that vastly exceed the computers at the disposal of large corporations or federal governments only twenty years ago. Even the once chalk-dusty, ivory-towered academics mocked so mercilessly by Kierkegaard and Nietzsche are now found in corporately minded, distance-learning, electronically wired postmodern multiversities (formerly known as universities). The metaphors of the information age rush in upon us at every turn. We casually speak of things today as processed, programmed, rebooted – education, art, thought, everything. Things are on the go with an unprecedented fury, speeding along like the universe itself, which, we are now told, is expanding at an ever-increasing rate of acceleration. Changes in the information technologies are taking place at an exponential rate of increase, as we double the speed of our processors and the memory capacity of microchips every couple of years (check out 'Moore's Law' on *Wikipedia*). We even begin to suspect that everything *is* information, exchanges of genetic information in living systems, exchanges of information among the micro-particles that make up the material world itself. Information is fast becoming our metaphysics, which is something Heidegger presciently pointed out back in the 1950s, even singling out the Anglo-American word 'information' as the culprit.[51]

More and more it looks like even *we* are information, which is why the present age does not shirk from calling itself 'post-human'. The post-human hovers over us like a looming, maybe even monstrous paradigm shift of such proportions as to make 'postmodern' look like small potatoes. We live on the border between the human and the spectre of the post-human. The post-humanists mean it. The horizons within which we have hitherto lived our lives, the unchanging genera which premodernity assured us were made by God, and the table of categories that modernity assured us were stable structures of pure Reason – birth and reproduction, ageing and death, body and mind, living and non-living, nature and culture, material and immaterial – are already being relentlessly destabilized, undergoing a radical shift, being fundamentally challenged, made to look porous and mutable under the pressure of info-techno-science.

Even the matter of the old nineteenth-century materialists begins to look a bit immaterial as theoretical physicists explore ever more deeply sub-atomic particles where the distinction between material and immaterial starts to get a little fuzzy. Physicists today propose ideas that in the past we would have expected to hear only from spirit-seers and mystagogues. They investigate the idea of alternate universes, meaning that the story currently being told from the Big Bang to oblivion might be merely *our* story, one story in the endless generation and destruction of universes, of universes endlessly spawning and being spawned by other universes.[52] They investigate multiple dimensions, maybe as many as eleven. Beyond 3D films and television, imagine a figure on a screen who would step out of the screen and into the cinema! If the mark of philosophy is supposed to be wonder, theoretical physicists threaten to steal the thunder of philosophy's wonder, almost daily proposing the most impossible things.

In the process, the fundamental horizons of human life, the paradigm of being 'human', is beginning to tremble as if in preparation for a deep mutation. We are investigating the elementary processes of our bodies in terms of the genetic information encoded in our DNA, the informational system that regulates our bodies, which has opened up a new world of genetic therapy. Stem-cell research envisages growing new organs to replace defective ones. The Methuselah Project, spearheaded by Cambridge scientist Aubrey de Grey (1963–), is hard at work on altering the breakdown of telomeres, which would mean extending life-expectancy into the centuries.[53] We are working on stunning ways of sustaining and altering life with biotechnological supplements, preventing disease, deferring death, more and more mingling the living body with non-living supplements. Our fragile flesh is being regularly reinforced with biotechnical replacement parts. Beyond handheld devices, we have begun to find ways to implant these digitalized devices in living bodies. Robots, once the province of science fiction, are making heady progress and steadily replacing human beings in the workplace, reminding us unnervingly of HAL in Stanley Kubrick's sci-fi classic *2001: A Space Odyssey*, the spaceship's mainframe computer, which becomes self-conscious and rises up against its human creators.

When Donna Haraway wrote 'A Manifesto for Cyborgs' (1985), she shocked a generation of humanists by making it clear that the rigid border between the living and the technological is disintegrating, that this opposition is porous and permeable. Indeed she described three 'border breakdowns': between the technological and the living, between human animals and non-human ones, and finally between material and immaterial, the ancient boundary lines patrolled so vigilantly by metaphysics and religion. The cyborg is a hybrid, a cybernetic organism, running together the human and the machine, ending the war between mind and body set off by Descartes. The cyborg is irreverent, a blasphemy, post-gender, and has no

Oedipus complex. It represents a dangerous trans-gression of boundaries.[54]

We have an acute sense of change and of the future, which presses in on us as never before as we are called upon to cease thinking of human life in terms of matter and spirit and to start thinking instead in terms of signals, neurons, digitalization and infor-mation. No wonder the new paradigm of the information revolution has spawned a whole new generation of post-human prophets, making post-modern prophets like Kierkegaard and Nietzsche look old-fashioned. Visit the website of Singularity University, where their futurists say the best way to predict the future is to invent it yourself.[55] The Singu-larity, as theorized by Ray Kurzweil, the author of *The Singularity is Near: When Humans Transcend Biology*, and the cofounder of the Singularity University, refers to that point when according to Moore's Law – he pre-dicts 2045 – the capacity of computers will overtake human intelligence. Then the computers will start designing the computers, and at that point he and others predict it will be possible to altogether separate life from its biological foundations. (As Kurzweil would be ninety-seven years old in 2045 he is currently popping a lot of vitamin pills to ensure he will be around for the ride.) Robotologists like Hans Moravec are hard at work on the project of upload-ing 'consciousness' – one of modernity's prized categories – and downloading it into shiny new robot 'bodies' (bodies without flesh) in which we could live on and on. At that point biological evolution will be capped by transcending biology altogether. Human transcendence will turn out to mean transcending the human. Talk about making the impossible possible! That would mark the information age as the end of the biological history of humankind and the beginning of the post-biological – whence post-human in the most literal sense.

Thus would the post-humanists attain, in a hitherto undreamt-of way, the ancient religious dream of immortality, so long as we stay out of the way of magnets and have safely stored a back-up copy of ourselves – like the resurrection ships in *Battlestar Galactica*. Finally, the futurists imagine taking leave of planet earth itself – talk about being on the go! – compared to which the shock delivered by the Copernican Revolution will elicit but a smile. I myself think that Moravec and Kurzweil are visiting us with another, perhaps more dazzling, digitalized version of Descartes' dualism of mind versus body. But these are serious and intelligent people, so even if we regard them as an outer fringe and write off all the stuff about uploading consciousness as science fiction (but remember, the first response to critical upheavals is scornful rejection, and the distinction between truth and fiction is not airtight), there is no denying the transformations of our lives that lie in store for us in the coming age of info-techno-science, and that are already rapidly changing everything. However it is assessed, the post-human, in some form or another, does not merely loom before us; it has already begun; it has already started its journey, its odyssey.

Now, just as postmodernists insist, nothing is unambiguous, and even this profound transformation is not immune to being given a religious interpretation (re-enter my frogs). Back in the first half of the twentieth century, Pierre Teilhard de Chardin (1881–1955), who was both a palaeontologist and a Jesuit priest, interpreted the history of evolution as the ascending complexification of consciousness.[56] This, he projected, would culminate in what he called the 'noosphere', meaning the gradual envelopment of the planet in a layer of thought, comparable to its envelopment in the layers of gases we call air. Teilhard had a kind of Hegelian streak to his thinking which led him to treat evolution as the evolving history of the Spirit, the enveloping of the planet in Spirit. Today it appears that something like Teilhard's projection is coming true, but not quite as he envisaged it. Teilhard thought this evolving noosphere would ultimately engender a Christo-sphere, enveloping the planet in what he called the Omega Point, the mind of Christ, who is both the Alpha and the Omega. Of course, instead of Christ, what we got was computers; instead of an atmosphere of Christ-consciousness, we got cloud computing. Today, a wireless information system is linking up distant places and people, weaving a light and airy blanket of info-technology over the face of the earth. This may very well allow for links to grow between people in an evolving common consciousness, but it also affords unprecedented powers of surveillance and control, not to mention a lot of lonely and isolated people seated in front of their computers.

Whatever we make of it, we stand at present on the border between a postmodern world, one that, however discontinuous its shifts and revolutions, has a continuity with its origins in the Greek and biblical culture that launched it, and a post-human one, an uncanny future in which life as we have known it will be transformed. In German, the word for uncanny is *unheimlich*, not-at-home, feeling strange and alienated and slightly spooked, which could not be more literally realized than in the spooky and unearthly projection of robot bodies and of establishing human colonies beyond planet earth. I have invoked the model of repetition and have treated the postmodern as a repetition of the premodern, which means the future is not only in front of us but can also be found behind us. But does that model still hold now, as we contemplate the post-human? Does the post-human repeat the human or just leave it behind? As Nietzsche's Zarathustra said, 'Man is a rope, tied between beast and Overman . . . What is the ape to a man? A laughing-stock, a thing of shame. And just so shall a man be to the Overman: a laughing-stock, a thing of shame.'[57] (We recall that Kubrick made reference to Nietzsche in *2001* by using Richard Strauss's 'Sunrise' from *Thus Spoke Zarathustra* as the musical theme of the film.) Is the discontinuity between the human and the post-human so great that repetition is impossible? Is the exploration of outer space a repetition of the exploration of the 'new world' undertaken by Europeans five hundred years ago or is it just plain unearthly? Do the advanced information technologies 'repeat' the birth of modern science four centuries ago, and was that not the repetition of the tools made by our prehistoric ancestors? Do the marvels of the new info-technology repeat the miracles of religion (healings, angelic messengers, resurrections, the mystical body of Christ, etc.)? Does the mystery of the universe, of the multiverse, repeat the mystery of what we call God? What will religion (our frogs) look like in the post-human world? Or politics? Or art? Do we stand before something truly unimaginable, utterly different? What will become of us? Where is this species going? These are the sorts of questions that philosophers of the future – not to mention everyone else – will face.

I began by describing a world in which we rush about the surface of our little planet, hurrying to work in the morning, hustling home at night, pushed and pulled in multiple directions, multi-tasked to the limits. Now I let the camera zoom out, far far out. The busy little planet circulates in a solar system that is itself off in the corner of a galaxy, off in the corner of the universe, which itself may be but one of many universes, as it speeds ahead to entropic dissipation. In the long run the sun will burn out and we will all have spoken dead languages. No one knows we are here.

Contemporary science has learned an enormous amount about the immensity of the universe without, as well as of the unimaginable minuteness of the sub-particles within. The universe is infinite without and infinitesimal within, leaving us to live our lives with the medium-sized objects in between, struggling with these unimaginable extremes in opposing orders of magnitude. The knowledge science has steadily acquired has exposed us all the more profoundly to the immensity of what we do not know. That is as it should be if truth, as I have argued, is the transition between truth and untruth; if truth comes to a head in openness to the not-yet true; if truth requires the risk of exposure to what we can't see coming. St Augustine once said, 'I have become a great question to myself' (*quaestio mihi magna factus sum*). He thought he knew all the answers when he set out to climb the ladder of the imperial Roman world, but after his conversion, after coming face to face with the mystery he called God, he was forced to confront the mystery within himself. Perhaps today the mystery of some unknowable immensity goes under another name – the universe, the multiverse, the cosmos, the chaosmos. It is impossible to know how far info-techno-science will take us, how little it will turn out science will have known in the present age, how long lifetimes can be extended, how utterly reproduction, ageing and death itself will be transformed, how many planets we will visit – provided the eventual advent of handheld nuclear weapons or some environmental disaster of our own doing does not first send us straight to oblivion.

A Postmodern Faith

This brings me back to religion, to my uncertain, irregular and heretical religion, religion being the test case of truth with which we started down this road. Now more than ever before we require faith, by which I mean not the beliefs of the confessional religions, which I think stand in need of a radical rethinking and are beginning to look excessively weary, but the postmodern faith in the event, the faith I have been describing, that the future is always better. I do not mean a confessional faith that is supposed to save us, but a more radical faith that puts us at risk. Now more than ever that faith will be put to the test. Perhaps the faith that is demanded of us now, that will be demanded of us in the future, will assume a more cosmic form, and we will have to give it words in some kind of cosmo-poetics, find a way to sing the song of the human condition that will take into account a stunning transformation in what we understand by the human. Perhaps everything we have thought and meant by philosophy and by truth will have been too earth-bound and will require a recontextualization – a repetition – in a more cosmic setting. Taken in such interstellar terms, we will see the event of human life on earth as a rare and precious moment when, for a few seconds of cosmic time, here and now, the cosmos burst into sensuous life and intelligence, in virtue of which a bit of the universe began to brood over itself and ask about its 'truth,' and as is the function of song, celebrated itself and gave thanks. Then the most ancient quality of philosophy, its provenance in wonder, will be repeated on a cosmic scale. Then the post-human will mean not the utter destruction of the human as we know it, but its repetition, its reinscription, its recontextualization on a cosmic stage.

Truth to tell, we do not know who we are – and that *is* who we are. That is the little kernel of wisdom, and the grain of truth, of faith in truth, I serve up as I seek to make a graceful exit from the stage. We *are* that non-knowing and my final thought, my plea, my prayer – I am always praying – is to let that non-knowing serve to temper all we know and to nourish a faith in the future. The more we learn, the more mysterious we learn we are. We are the ones who wonder where we are going, travellers all and always, *homo viator*, always under way. We are a little place (perhaps just one of many) in the universe where the universe (perhaps itself just one of many) has reserved a space to do its thinking, to worry and to marvel over itself under the little name of truth. Remember the uncanny scene evoked by the young Nietzsche, who mocked the little animals off in a remote corner of the universe who invented proud words like 'truth', after which the universe moved on and the little animals had to die. I find that an occasion not only for a salutary mockery of our anthropocentrism, as did Nietzsche, but also for wonder that this vast universe should for a moment have made room for a bit of thought and language, a bit of joy and wonder, a bit of invention. The wonders are everywhere, beginning with the sub-atomic particles in our bodies, which we are told are of ancient cosmic origin, millions of years old. We are such stuff as the stars are made of. We are stardust and unto stardust we shall return. That is at least one immortality we will be granted.

As the motto of my hermeneutics is that we get the best results by facing up to the worst, I find a strange joy in all this non-knowing, and I experience a sense of gratitude for a gift I didn't ask to be given, for a purely gratuitous existence coming from I know not where and headed somewhere I cannot foresee, in short, for an event. The mystery is all around us and within us. If we think of life as a journey, then it is the joy of the journey that matters and we are in no hurry to get to the final destination. We are a bit of cosmic luck, of fortuitousness, which means that life is a grace. That is why it is so grievous when life is squandered or cut short, whether by misfortune or human malice. Grace is natural before it is supernatural and it is supernatural only because it is natural, 'supernatural' being best viewed as a hyperbole or a compliment, a way we have of saying how blessed we are by it. Grace happens; it is an event. We don't need God for grace, but we do need grace for God, 'God' being one of the ways we have devised to say, to sing, to express our gratitude for grace, for such felicity as things permit, with or without what is called God in religion. Grace is one of those high-velocity words, words of elemental power and promise by which we give names to the event, to what is happening to us.

Back one last time to my primal scene, where a certain Augustine still converses into the early hours with a rogue who rightly passes for an atheist. The two are both philosophers so long as 'philosophers' means 'lovers'. The word is otherwise not an exact fit for either one of them, these lovers of tears, these restless hearts, whose *cor inquietum* is their common constitution. For them to philosophize, if that is what they do, is a matter of love, and truth is something to make, to do, and it is risky business, not a bit reassuring. It should be clear by now that when I speak of a certain odd and irregular 'religion' or of 'loving truth' I am not being comforting or sentimental; I am talking about negotiating an abyss. In the scene I am always staging, Augustine and Derrida both confess a secret, the one to the other, that they do not know the truth of their desire, that they do not know in truth what they love and desire when they love and desire their God. But that non-knowing does not spell the end of their desire; it is precisely what drives desire forward, sparking in them a desire beyond desire. The two are separated by an accident of birth – a French avant-garde writer who sometimes says insouciant and heretical things and an ancient bishop-theologian with a short fuse for heretics. But they are still more joined by this same accident – not only the same homeland, the same journey across the Mediterranean, but the same confessional or circumfessional heart. The one calls this accident a 'grace', a *tolle-lege* game of God's gracious beneficence; the other calls it an 'event', a poker game of events, a bit of cosmic chance.

Everything I mean by truth happens here: the *truth* of their difference takes place in the non-knowing. The *truth* is lodged in the untruth they both confess, to which they are both exposed, making truth a matter of exposure not of propositions, of painful, prayerful, tearful openness. They are torn open by the force of truth, driven to a point where neither we nor they can tell the difference between the event of grace and the grace of an event, and this because 'grace' and 'event' are but differing beliefs that dissolve in the depths of a darker faith. The *truth* is that these two seekers are compatriots, as are we all – all siblings of the same dark night of unfathomable truth, of a truth still to come.

Suggestions for Further Reading

The sources of the debates western philosophers have conducted about truth are to be found among the Greeks. See the philosophical poem written by the Greek philosopher Parmenides of Elea (born *c.* 515 BCE) which can be found in G. S. Kirk, J. E. Raven and M. Schofield, *The Presocratic Philosophers*, 2nd edition (Cambridge: Cambridge University Press, 1983). The other must-read text is Plato's *Republic*, Books V–VII in particular. The translation by Benjamin Jowett is in the public domain and can be found online. There are any number of superb essays by the leading authorities of the day on Augustine in *A Companion to Augustine*, ed. Mark Vessey (Oxford: Wiley-Blackwell Publishing, 2012). The best popular expositions of Augustine that are also highly reliable are those by Gary Wills. For more on Augustine's relation to Derrida, see *Augustine and Postmodernism: Confessions and Circumfession*, ed. John D. Caputo and Michael Scanlon (Bloomington: Indiana University Press, 2005). The high point of the medieval discussion of truth is to be found in Thomas Aquinas, a good sampling of whose works is collected in *An*

Aquinas Reader: Selections from the Writings of Thomas Aquinas, ed. Mary T. Clark (New York: Fordham University Press, 2000). Mary Clark is also a very reliable expositor of Augustine.

The notes on pp. 267–75 contain references to the philosophical works consulted in the early modern period and the nineteenth century, and there are many excellent guides to this period. One of the older but still popular and reliable studies of this period (and to the entire history of philosophy, but I think it gets better as it goes on) is the history of philosophy by Frederick Copleston, an English Jesuit who taught at Heythrop College: *A History of Philosophy*, 9 volumes (London: Burns, Oates & Washbourne, 1958–75). One very good way into Kierkegaard is to interweave his biography and his work, which is masterfully done in Alastair Hannay, *Kierkegaard: A Biography* (Cambridge: Cambridge University Press, 2001). The same thing can be said of Nietzsche, and here I recommend R. J. Hollingdale, *Nietzsche: The Man and His Philosophy*, 2nd edition (Cambridge: Cambridge University Press, 2001). As for Derrida, the Peeters biography (see note 13) is very helpful. Derrida has expounded a conception of truth in connection with an interpretation of Nietzsche in *Spurs: Nietzsche's Styles / Eperons: Les Styles de Nietzsche*, French text with English trans. by Barbara Harlow (Chicago: University of Chicago Press, 1987); but this text is very difficult. A contemporary classic, perhaps the most basic thing to read to gain entrance to the continental discussions of truth, is Martin Heidegger's 'On the Essence of Truth', in *Heidegger: Basic Writings*, ed. David F. Krell, 2nd edition (New York: Harper & Row, 1993), which is overall a superb collection.

For a lucid approach to truth that focuses on propositional truth (whose importance I do wish to underestimate) while assuming the worst about the postmodernists – treating them as relativists – see Harry Frankfurt, *On Truth* (New York: Alfred Knopf, 2006), which is a sequel to his *On Bullshit* (Princeton: Princeton University Press, 2005), which is also very much worth reading. At the other end of this spectrum, Richard Rorty defended the pragmatist idea that truth is nothing more than a compliment we pay to sentences that are paying their own way in his now classic *Philosophy and the Mirror of Nature* (Princeton: Princeton University Press, 1979).

The question of truth and religion in modernity, which I used as my test case for the mutation that takes place in truth, is discussed with much acumen, although at rather great length, in Charles Taylor, *A Secular Age* (Cambridge, Mass.: Belknap Press, 2007). For the latest version of the debate between faith and reason today, see Jürgen Habermas and Joseph Ratzinger (Pope Benedict XVI), *The Dialectics of Secularization: On Reason and Religion* (San Francisco: Ignatius Press, 2007). Habermas is arguably Europe's most distinguished defender of the Enlightenment project today and the leading figure of the 'Frankfurt School', headed by Adorno and Horkheimer, which is looking for a way out of the disenchantment described by Weber.

To see in the concrete what I mean by religious truth as a form of life rather than as a body of doctrines or propositions that correspond to supernatural facts of the matter, I can think of nothing better than two novels by Marilynne Robinson: *Gilead: A Novel* (New York: Picador, 2004) and *Home* (New York: Farrar, Straus and Giroux, 2008).

Notes

1. Jean-François Lyotard, *The Postmodern Condition: A Report on Knowledge*, trans. Geoff Bennington and Brian Massumi (Minneapolis: University of Minnesota Press, 1984), pp. xxiii–xxv. While this is the most commonly cited 'definition' of the postmodern, not every postmodern writer signs up to it.

2. With this expression, I am running together Ecclesiastes and Andy Warhol.

3. Cited in *Kierkegaard's Writings*, XII, *Concluding Unscientific Postscript to 'Philosophical Fragments'*, trans. and ed. Howard and Edna Hong (Princeton: Princeton University Press, 1992), p. 106.

4. *The Confessions of St Augustine*, trans. Rex Warner (New York: Penguin Books, 1963), Bk I, c. 1, p. 17.

5. Michel Foucault, *History of Madness*, ed. Jean Khalfa, trans. Jonathan Murphy (Oxford: Routledge, 2006).

6. The most common theory of truth among philosophers is the 'correspondence' theory, that an assertion ('S is p') pictures or picks out (corresponds to) a fact out in the world (an 'Sp').

7. See 'Science as a Vocation', in *From Max Weber: Essays in Sociology*, ed. H. H. Gerth and C. Wright Mills (Oxford: Routledge, 1948), p. 129 ff.

8. Max Horkheimer and Theodor Adorno, *Dialectic of Enlightenment*, ed. Gunzelin Schmid Noerr, trans. Edmund Jephcott (Stanford: Stanford University Press, 2007).

9. 'Religion is the sigh of the oppressed creature, the heart of a heartless world, and the soul of soulless conditions. It is the opium of the people.' Karl Marx, 'Introduction' to *A Contribution to the Critique of Hegel's Philosophy of Right*, ed. Joseph O'Malley (Cambridge: Cambridge University Press, 1970), p. 171.

10. Michel Foucault, *The Courage of the Truth: The Government of Self and Others*, trans. Graham Burchell (Basingstoke: Palgrave Macmillan, 2012). Foucault wants to retrieve the virtue of truth-telling under the ancient name of *parrhesia*, which we can roughly translate as 'telling all', 'letting it all hang out'.

11. Paul Tillich, *Dynamics of Faith* (San Francisco: HarperOne, 2001).

12. J. L. Austin, *How to Do Things with Words* (Oxford: Clarendon, 1962).

13. For more on Derrida's life, see Benoit Peeters, *Derrida: A Biography*, trans. Andrew Brown (Cambridge: Polity Press, 2012).

14. *Confessions*, Bk VIII, c. 12, pp. 182–3.

15. Jacques Derrida, 'Circumfession: Fifty-nine Periods and Periphrases', in Geoffrey Bennington and Jacques Derrida, *Jacques Derrida*, trans. Geoffrey Bennington (Chicago: University of Chicago Press, 1993).

16. Jean-Louis Chrétien, 'The Wounded Word: The Phenomenology of Prayer', trans. Jeff Kosky, in *Phenomenology*

and the 'Theological Turn': The French Debate, eds. Dominique Janicaud et al. (New York: Fordham University Press, 2001).

17. Martin Heidegger, *Being and Time*, trans. John Macquarrie and Edward Robinson (New York: Harper & Row, 1962), §§74–6, pp. 434–49.

18. Martin Heidegger, 'On the Essence of Truth', in *Heidegger: Basic Writings*, ed. David F. Krell, 2nd edn (New York: Harper & Row, 1993), pp. 111–38.

19. See Alain Badiou, *Saint Paul: The Foundation of Universalism*, trans. Ray Brassier (Stanford: Stanford University Press, 2003); Slavoj Žižek, *The Puppet and the Dwarf: The Perverse Core of Christianity* (Cambridge, Mass.: MIT Press, 2003); Slavoj Žižek, *The Fragile Absolute – or Why the Christian Legacy is Worth Fighting For* (London: Verso, 2000).

20. Of the many editions available, I have always liked René Descartes, *Meditations on First Philosophy*, trans. Laurence J. Lafleur (Indianapolis and New York: Bobbs-Merrill, Library of Liberal Arts, 1960).

21. 'Do not go abroad. Return within yourself. In the inward man truth dwells.' ('*Noli foras ire, in te ipsum redi, in interiore homine habitat.*') 'Of True Religion', in *Augustine: Earlier Writings*, trans. John Burleigh (Philadelphia: Westminster Press, 1953), c. xxix, 72, p. 262.

22. Ray Kurzweil, *The Singularity is Near: When Humans Transcend Biology* (New York: Penguin, 2005).

23. The sentence is found in the Preface to the Second Edition of the *Critique of Pure Reason*, trans. Norman Kemp

Smith (London: Macmillan, 1963), p. 29. There is no better introduction to Kant than this Preface. The *Foundations of the Metaphysics of Morals*, trans. Lewis White Beck (Indianapolis and New York: Bobbs-Merrill, Library of Liberal Arts, 1960) is a slightly more readable version of his ethics.

24. Immanuel Kant, *Religion Within the Limits of Reason Alone*, trans. T. M. Greene and H. H. Hudson (New York: Harper & Bros., 1960), p. 90 ff.

25. True to the postmodern hypothesis that nothing is simple, one could read Kant against Kant, by taking into account his idea of the 'sublime', which is a representation of the unrepresentable, as when we try to imagine the unimaginable vastness of the universe, and thereby produce a postmodern Kant. But that would take us down another track and off on a long detour.

26. There are texts of Hegel that you would never forgive me for recommending to your reading; they are that difficult. In general it is better to stick with his lectures, which are relatively clear. My favourites include the three 'Introductions' to the lectures on art, religion and philosophy conveniently collected in G. W. F. Hegel, *On Art, Religion, Philosophy*, ed. J. Glenn Gray (New York: Harper Torchbooks, 1970).

27. Friedrich Nietzsche, *Twilight of the Idols*, trans. R. J. Hollingdale (Harmondsworth: Penguin Classics, 1973), Part One, pp. 15–36.

28. Kierkegaard, *Concluding Unscientific Postscript*, p. 186.

29. The best work on Kierkegaard and the city has been done by George Pattison, *'Poor Paris!': Kierkegaard's Critique of the Spectacular City* (Berlin and New York: Walter de Gruyter, 1999) and *Kierkegaard and the Quest for the Unambiguous Life* (Oxford: Oxford University Press, 2013).

30. Kierkegaard, *Concluding Unscientific Postscript*, p. 286.

31. Alastair Hannay, *Søren Kierkegaard: Papers and Journals: A Selection*, trans. Alastair Hannay (London and New York: Penguin Books, 1996), pp. 32–3.

32. *Kierkegaard's Writings*, XIV, *Two Ages: The Age of Revolution and the Present Age*, trans. and ed. Howard and Edna Hong (Princeton: Princeton University Press, 1978).

33. Kierkegaard, *Concluding Unscientific Postscript*, pp. 189–204.

34. *Kierkegaard's Writings*, VI, *Fear and Trembling* and *Repetition*, trans. and ed. Howard and Edna Hong (Princeton: Princeton University Press, 1983).

35. Friedrich Nietzsche, *The Birth of Tragedy and Other Writings*, Cambridge Texts in the History of Philosophy, ed. Raymond Geuss and Ronald Speirs (Cambridge: Cambridge University Press, 1999).

36. 'On the Truth and Lies in the Nonmoral Sense', in *Philosophy and Truth: Selections from Nietzsche's Notebooks of the Early 1870s*, ed. and trans. Daniel Breazeale (Atlantic Highlands, NJ: Humanities Press, 1979), p. 84. For a good presentation of Nietzsche's views on truth, see Friedrich Nietzsche, *Beyond Good and Evil*, trans. R. J. Hollingdale (Harmondsworth: Penguin Classics, 1968), ch. 3.

37. For Nietzsche's critique of Socrates, see *Twilight of the Idols*, ch. 2, pp. 29–34.

38. Friedrich Nietzsche, *Thus Spoke Zarathustra*, trans. Walter Kaufmann (New York: Viking Press, 1966).

39. Friedrich Nietzsche, *Ecce Homo*, trans. R. J. Hollingdale (Harmondsworth: Penguin Classics, 1968), pp. 69–81.

40. Nietzsche, 'On the Truth and Lies', p. 79.

41. The charter statement of contemporary hermeneutics is Heidegger's *Being and Time*, §§31–3, 45, 61; its most famous presentation is Hans-Georg Gadamer, *Truth and Method*, 2nd rev. edn, trans. Joel Weinsheimer and Donald G. Marshall (New York: Crossroad, 1991).

42. The contemporary philosopher from whom we have the most to learn about the lines of communication among Hermes, angels and smartphones is Michel Serres, whose many works I warmly recommend.

43. That is the first big story about Truth that we were told by an early Greek thinker named Parmenides, who left his mark on Plato and thereby on the entire subsequent tradition of philosophy. The goddess steered Parmenides along the path of unchanging immortal truth and away from the changeable paths of mortals. In my view, philosophers ever since have been trying to dig out from under that tall tale.

44. Ludwig Wittgenstein, *Philosophical Investigations*, trans. G. E. M. Anscombe (Oxford: Blackwell, 1951, 2001).

45. Thomas Kuhn, *The Structure of Scientific Revolutions*, 4th edn, with an Introduction by Ian Hacking (Chicago:

University of Chicago Press, 1962, 2012). As with Wittgenstein, I am citing the Fiftieth Anniversary edition.

46. Imre Lakatos, *Criticism and the Growth of Knowledge* (Cambridge: Cambridge University Press, 1972).

47. *Time* Magazine, 23 July 23 2012, p. 35. The 'standard model' of particle physics is the prevailing view in physics, built up over the last seventy years or so, which explains why the universe is not simply a field of particles without mass moving about at the speed of light but is instead made of atoms, molecules, people, planets, stars, etc. It explains how elementary particles (fermions) interact by exchanging energy (bosons) with one other. The Higgs boson, which was predicted by the standard model but only recently confirmed, explains how particles gather mass. See Dennis Overbye, 'Chasing the Higgs', *New York Times* 'Science Times', 5 March 2013, and Brian Greene, *The Elegant Universe* (New York: Norton, 2003), pp. 123, 198, 381.

48. I do not deny that I am doing a certain amount of hermeneutic violence to Kuhn. Kuhn thought that invoking the word truth caused an unnecessary complication in interpreting the work of science, and that it was enough to think in terms of successfully solving the problems that arise within and between paradigms. I myself think it better to say that he was redescribing truth, that he touched on the event of truth, on the shock that truth delivers and the lure or pull of truth that draws us on, and that it is an unnecessary complication to pit paradigms and truth against each other. In

order to sink our teeth into reality, we need both reality and teeth, and paradigms are our teeth.

49. See Ian Hacking, *The Social Construction of What?* (Cambridge, Mass.: Harvard University Press, 2001); and Bruno Latour, *Pandora's Hope: Essays on the Reality of Science Studies* (Cambridge, Mass.: Harvard University Press, 1999).

50. In John D. Caputo, *The Weakness of God: A Theology of the Event* (Bloomington: Indiana University Press, 2006), I do exactly that, put God on the side of the revolutionary shock of the event.

51. Martin Heidegger, *The Principle of Reason*, trans. Reginald Lily (Bloomington: Indiana University Press, 1991), p. 29. Unfortunately, Heidegger had a reactionary attitude towards contemporary technology and famously declared that 'science does not think'. Today, Heidegger and the generation of luminaries of postmodern thinking (Derrida, Foucault, Lyotard, Deleuze), all of whom belonged to the previous century and are now dead, are taking fire from a new brand of modernism, materialism and realism, which charge them with failing to think though what is going on in the contemporary mathematical physical sciences. This movement is spearheaded by Quentin Meillassoux; see his *After Finitude*, trans. Ray Brassier (London: Continuum, 2008). For a critical appreciation of this movement, permit me to refer to John D. Caputo, *The Insistence of God: A Theology of Perhaps* (Bloomington: Indiana University Press, 2013).

52. See Paul J. Steinhardt and Neil Turok, *Endless Universe: Beyond the Big Bang—Rewriting Cosmic History* (New York: Doubleday, 2007).

53. See Aubrey de Grey, *Ending Aging: The Rejuvenation Breakthroughs That Could Reverse Human Aging in Our Lifetime* (New York: St Martin's Griffin, 2008). If we think of chromosomes as shoestrings and of telomeres as their ends, then the way to prevent ageing is to prevent the ends from unravelling.

54. Donna Haraway, 'A Manifesto for Cyborgs: Science, Technology, and Socialist Feminism in the 1980s', in *The Haraway Reader* (New York: Routledge, 2004), pp. 7–46.

55. See www.singularityu.org, the website of Singularity University, founded by Ray Kurzweil and Peter Diamandis; see also Kurzweil, *The Singularity is Near*.

56. Pierre Teilhard de Chardin, *The Phenomenon of Man* (New York: Harper Perennial Modern Classics, 2008). Teilhard was deeply influenced by the vitalism of Henri Bergson (1859–1941).

57. Nietzsche, *Thus Spoke Zarathustra*, pp. 3–4.

Index

Philosophy in Transit

This new series of short, accessible books by some of the world's leading philosophers sheds light on how the idea of transit has changed what we think about fundamentals such as truth and self.

Each takes on a major theme from the history of philosophy, as well as current philosophical debate. What does truth mean in this age of hyper mobility? How has the movement of digital information altered our sense of the self? Contemporary philosophical themes are also considered, including: what is an event? Or, why grow up?

Using various modes of transportation (either real, virtual or otherwise) as their starting point, each thinker offers a lively, original and personal work of philosophy about the non-stop reality of modern life, allowing readers to think about what it really means to get around.

Truth	*Self*
John D. Caputo	Barry Dainton
Event	*Why Grow Up?*
Slavoj Žižek	Susan Neiman

Event
Slavoj Žižek

What is really happening when something happens?

In the second in a new series of accessible, commute-length books of original thought, Slavoj Žižek, one of the world's greatest living philosophers, examines the new and highly-contested concept of Event.

An Event can be an occurrence that shatters ordinary life, a radical political rupture, the emergence of a religious belief, the rise of a new art form, or an intense experience such as falling in love. After an event, nothing remains the same even if there are no obvious large changes.

Taking us on a trip which stops at different definitions of Event, Žižek addresses fundamental questions such as: How much are we agents of our own fates? Which conditions must be met for us to perceive something as really existing? In a world that's constantly changing, is anything new really happening?

Drawing on references from Plato to arthouse cinema, the Big Bang to Buddhism, *Event* is a journey into philosophy at its most exciting and elementary.

Published in January 2014

Self
Barry Dainton

When you think 'What am I?', what's actually doing the thinking?

Is it a soul, some other kind of mental entity separate from your body, or are 'you' just a collection of nerve-endings and narratives?

In the third in a new series of short, provoking books of original philosophy, acclaimed thinker Barry Dainton takes us through the nature of Self and its relation to the rest of reality.

Starting his journey with Descartes' claim that we are non-physical beings (even if it seems otherwise), and Locke's view that a person is self-conscious matter (though not necessarily in human form), Dainton explores how today's rapid movement of people and information affects our understanding of self. When technology re-configures our minds, will it remake us, or kill us? If teleportation becomes possible, would it be rational to use it? Could we achieve immortality by uploading ourselves into virtual worlds?

Far-reaching and witty, *Self* is a spirited exploration of the idea that in a constantly changing world, we and our bodies can go their separate ways.

Published in May 2014

Why Grow Up?
Susan Neiman

**Becoming an adult today
can seem a grim prospect.**

As you grow up, you are told to renounce most of the dreams of your youth and resign yourself to an existence that is a pale dilution of the adventurous, important and enjoyable life you once expected. But who wants to do that? No wonder we live in a culture of rampant immaturity, argues renowned philosopher Susan Neiman.

In *Why Grow Up*, the fourth in a series of short books of original thought, Neiman shows how philosophy can help us want to grow up. Travel, both literally and metaphorically, has been seen as a crucial step to coming of age by thinkers as diverse as Kant, Rousseau and Simone de Beauvoir. Neiman asks how this idea can help us build a new model of maturity.

Refuting the widespread belief that the best time of your life is between sixteen and twenty-six, she argues that being grown-up is an ideal worth striving for.

Published in September 2014